N

Written Off

NOT
Written Off

Best Wishes

Marion Hughes.

x

Marion Hughes

© Marion Hughes, 2017

Published by Backworth Publishing

thebookmh@yahoo.com

A CIP catalogue record for this book is available from the British Library.

ISBN 978-0-9955842-0-4

Book layout and cover design by Clare Brayshaw

Cover image ©Naufalmq | Dreamstime.com
(Lonely girl with teddy bear in hand photo)

Prepared and printed by:

York Publishing Services Ltd
64 Hallfield Road
Layerthorpe
York YO31 7ZQ

Tel: 01904 431213

Website: www.yps-publishing.co.uk

Not Written Off

I was really still a baby when I was taken into care.
Mother died quite suddenly, leaving my father in despair.
For months he tried to manage keeping us at home.
But he couldn't cope being left with ten children all alone.
Then at just eleven I was told 'your Dad is dead.'
With no one to answer questions running through my head.
I'd only got to know my dad, when I was eight years old.
My treasured memories with him are the ones I dearly hold.
Living in an orphanage, had many ups and downs.
But my strength and resilience, taught me not to frown.
I was 'Written off' at eighteen, an unfortunate way to say.
We are no longer liable, so you'd best be on your way.

The Author as a baby (1949)

Contents

	Introduction	ix
1	Visiting My Past	1
2	Stepping Inside	4
3	Family History	9
4	Mount Royal	15
5	Bedtime	22
6	School Mornings	28
7	Infant School	34
8	Mams and Dads	43
9	Lost Time	46
10	Junior School	50
11	Secondary School	54
12	Ouch	63
13	Nitti Nora	68
14	Saturdays	70
15	Sundays	87
16	Indoor Activities	96
17	Outdoor Activities	106
18	Long Walks	112
19	The Shoe Cupboard	120

20	Home Visits	126
21	Your Dad is Dead	139
22	Christmas Preparations	147
23	Christmas Time	154
24	Beyond the Walls	162
25	Tribute to Dad	173
26	Reflections	175
27	Acknowledgements	178

Introduction

I may have been 'written off' Barnardo's books at the age of eighteen, but my childhood experiences have never been erased from my memory and have had a profound effect on the adult I have become.

Living in a world of children without parents meant I was blissfully unaware my mother had died when I was eighteen months old and that I was actually the youngest of ten children. The first inkling that my childhood was different to other children came whilst playing with friends at infant school, they referred to a 'Mam and Dad.' These were words I had not heard before.

Physically I was well looked after, given three square meals a day and was always well-clothed and presented. However, at eleven years old I struggled to cope with the traumatic news that my Dad was dead and I felt there was no emotional support for me.

Until I received a copy of my archived records from Barnardo's I had no prior knowledge of my family history. The circumstances for my placement into the Orphanage had never been discussed with me by any of my immediate family or, by a member of staff at the home. I also refer to new found information about myself discovered in my archived records which astonished me.

Despite living within a very strict regime by today's standards of care, my unique childhood experiences were also filled with laughter. I have many happy memories of the friendships and communal bond I shared with my peers.

In this book I set out to write about my own personal experiences of my upbringing within an orphanage and at no time do I reflect the views of my siblings or any other residents.

1

Visiting My Past

One Saturday afternoon, my sister and I decided to revisit 'Mount Royal', a magnificent building which had been the orphanage we had lived in many years previously. We knew the house now belonged to a private owner but had no idea who the occupants were or if they would mind strangers knocking on their door.

It had been more than fifty years since we had last meandered up the long gravelled driveway. We glanced at the vast, rambling garden. The trees and shrubs had grown beyond recognition since we had last seen them. We reminisced about those carefree days of the past when we played in the grounds for many hours running and skipping or climbing trees until the sound of the bell rang out at mealtimes.

The boundary wall looked so much smaller now. Many years ago, we'd needed to help each other to climb up and sit on that very same wall. We'd sit there for hours, whiling away the time and waving at the occasional passing car. We often saw horse drawn ornate gypsy caravans passing by and wondered how a whole family could live in such a small space.

As we reached the grand entrance of the huge stone house, a white haired gentleman appeared from the rear of the building. Crossing the pathway to our immediate right, he disappeared into a large green shed, closing the door behind him. Increasing my pace, I nervously approached the shed with my sister one step behind me.

I gently knocked at the door and waited. There was no reply. Sis prodded me in the back, pushing me forward. I knocked again, louder this time. The gentleman slowly opened the door a short way. 'Yes?' he said in a quiet voice.

'Excuse me sir, we are trespassers, we lived here as orphans fifty years ago.' His eyes lit up, his face shone with the broadest smile as he opened the door wider and stepped outside. 'Oh!' He exclaimed. 'My son will be so pleased to meet you' he said, as he grasped my hand in both of his. He then closed the door behind him, and started walking towards the building he had emerged from.

Sis and I looked at each other, jaws dropped. He turned and beckoned us to follow him. We headed towards a building we knew as The Ballroom. The room was now modernised into luxurious accommodation for the parents of the current owners.

The gentleman introduced us to his wife as he reached for the phone to call his son. With urgency in his voice, he asked 'Where are you? We have visitors from the past.' Placing the phone back on its stand, he excitedly informed us, 'They are only five minutes away.'

After a short time, we heard the familiar sound from our past, of car tyres rumbling on the gravel driveway. Two adults and two children emerged from the car and with outreached arms they approached us. 'How nice to meet you, we are delighted you decided to visit us. We are very interested in the history of our house.

'Do come in.'

2

Stepping Inside

Stepping inside the door, I was surprised at the incredible emotion welling up inside me. The circular vestibule flooring and woodwork in the grand hallway were exactly as I remembered. I had that overwhelming feeling of peace and contentment, of coming home.

The owners kindly took us into every room of their house. We chatted and described how each room had been decorated when we lived there. It was amazing and pleasing to see that structurally very little had changed. The beautiful parquet flooring and the fireplaces had been preserved.

What had been our dining room was now a comfortable snug and music room. Our noisy playing room, where we played board games, dominoes, and did jigsaws, was now a lovely dining room. Their lounge had been our quiet area, for the children doing embroidery or knitting, or those who wanted to just have a quiet conversation.

It's so strange how the memory works. Bringing back all the past hustle and bustle that went on in those rooms. The first thing I remembered was the swishing sound the metal roller track made in both of these rooms, as the curtains were opened and closed in the huge bay windows.

The kitchen had been modernised, but I found it unbelievable that what appeared to be the very same pulley from all those years ago was still attached to the ceiling above the now, more modern Aga. The memories of us queuing up for hot chocolate after bath time came flooding back.

Thankfully, the doorway to the scary office was now boarded up, if you were summoned there, it meant trouble. I quickly passed that area before any of my bad experiences surfaced. The stairs were slightly different. The banister rail was now more open, with wooden spindles. It had been boxed in when we lived there. I was so happy to see that beautiful stained-glassed landing window, positioned at the bend of the stairway, was still there. Walking through the landing area, we headed towards what had been the girls' dormitories and shared bathroom.

The dormitories were unrecognisable. We remembered the walls being painted pale green with matching counterpanes on the beds. Both dorms had a large bay window at the front and a smaller straight side window. The two side windows of the bays were kept open from first thing in the morning until bedtime. The metal-framed, hospital-type beds were positioned along both of the side walls, with just enough room for a wooden chair between each bed.

All the curtains were made from the same batch of material with colourful flowers, which brightened up what could have been very dull rooms. The walls of both dormitories had been bare, except for the fireplace walls which were adorned with two pictures.

One picture was of a small child standing underneath a fruit tree, the other was a picture of Jesus with his eyes staring forward. I found that picture to be particularly scary at first, because it didn't matter where you were standing in the room or when you looked at it, the eyes were always staring in your direction.

I recalled a time when one of the girls asked a member of staff how and, why this happened. She was told it was because Jesus was keeping watch over us. Some of the girls took that to mean he was like a Guardian Angel but, others thought he was a spy, keeping an eye on us, checking we were behaving ourselves. If I was being mischievous, I would check to see if he was watching. As predicted, he was. I didn't think he was spying though. I found it reassuring to know someone was watching over us.

The bathroom had been a large, cold, open plan-area, almost the same size as a dormitory. Entering the door, there used to be a long strip of wood with brass hooks on the left-hand side of the wall. A child's name was beside each hook so we could hang our own multi striped towel and face cloths on when we had finished using them. Well, not actually our own towels, we used them for a whole week, Saturday to Saturday.

During our early years living there, a large white cast-iron bath stood behind the door to the right and two small wash basins mounted on the wall at the base of the bath, to the far right beside a window which seemed to be forever open, stood the single toilet. Looking straight ahead, under yet another open window stood a large painted bookcase with our coloured beakers, tooth brush and tooth paste standing on the shelves. These facilities were used by all age groups of girls sleeping in the two dormitories.

There was no such thing as privacy. A girl could be sitting on the toilet while others bathed or cleaned their teeth.

Thankfully, the bathroom was eventually partitioned. I found it strange to see that the now luxuriously modernised bathroom, had the partitions in the same position.

As we were shown around, the family listened to our stories about what life had been like for us. Passing back through the landing we explained the use of the huge floor to ceiling fitted cupboards and told them how, all those years ago, I had believed the landing cupboards to be a real Aladdin's cave where clothes mysteriously appeared. And, that if a bus load of ladies from regional WI's were scheduled to visit us on an afternoon during the school holidays, we were ordered to get changed out of our comfortable well-worn, playing-out clothes, into a smarter outfit and if anyone dared complain, one of the staff would shout,

'You may be Orphans but you don't have to look like one. So you don't.'

Some children got upset at her remarks, but I found her comments quite amusing, probably because she was right, and of course, I had heard her say that so many times before. They opened one of the doors for us to see the evidence of our existence. To our amazement and delight, some of the shelves still had the labels stuck in them for sheets and pillowcases.

We shared our happy memories of time spent playing in the ballroom especially during our ballroom and country dancing lessons.

Our spontaneous visit to Mount Royal was an incredible experience. We were warmly welcomed and shared so many stories about our time living there. With the excitement of the day still whirling in my head, I was inspired to write this poem and set about capturing my memories on paper.

Mount Royal

I love Mount Royal, wall to wall; it means so much to me.
Once owned by Barnardo's with a very strict regime.
I lived in that orphanage from 1951 until 1963.
Yes, there were moments when life could be quite fraught.
But today I am so grateful for all that I was taught.
I learned to sew, to sing and dance and care for one another.
Barnardo's really saved my life when I lost my mother.
Recently revisiting to recall my years gone by,
The warmth of my greeting made me want to cry.
I am at peace with myself as happy as can be.
Mount Royal is the foundation of whom I've grown to be.

3

Family History

The Thompson family lived at 6, Castle Square, Backworth, in a three bedroomed semi-detached council house. Dad was a coal miner, working a full range of shifts down the local pit while Mam stayed at home to look after their ten children born between 1931 and 1947. All seemed to be well until my mam became unwell and died unexpectedly on 31st October 1948 aged just thirty nine years.

Many years later my eldest sister Audrey, who was just fourteen years old at the time of my mother's death, told me that Mam had complained of having a headache, then, became unconscious. The local doctor was called and she was taken to the RVI Hospital in Newcastle where she died a few days later.

I clearly remember Audrey telling me that our Mam had died of hardening of the arteries but, the cause of death on her Death Certificate states she died of Pneumonia and Bronchitis. I have often wondered if the fact my mother gave birth to ten children within sixteen years was partially responsible for her early death.

My Barnardo's records state that Dad, also just thirty nine years old, struggled with the formidable task of going to work and coping on his own with ten children.

As there was no immediate family close by to help out, dad needed to take time off work to look after us. The eldest child of the family, Robert, was 16 at the time and had already left home to work on a local farm. Still living at home, there was Audrey 14, Matthew 12, Olive 10, Thomas 9, June 7, Albert 6, Ethel May 4, Douglas 2 and myself, Marion, 19 months old.

The local policeman reported the family situation to the NSPCC:

Father is finding it difficult to attend work and also keeping eldest daughter Audrey off school to run the place, he spends too much time and money at that local Club womanising. So if the children were taken into care he could make a contribution.

The local Policeman and a NSPCC officer visited my father at home to assess the family situation. The NSPCC officer then sent a report of his findings to Barnardo's dated November 1948:

I am satisfied that there is no neglect. Home is reasonable, but definitely the father could not give full attention to such a large family, and go out to work.

Since the mother died the father was finding it very difficult to give the children the full and proper attention they needed. The eldest girl has been kept off school. All appeared to be strong looking youngsters. Fairly well dressed, but the girls were wearing thin frocks.

If the Management could accept the candidates, we would like the boys to be kept together as they get along very well and never argue among themselves. This also applies to the girls.

Father works down a coal mine earning a wage of £7.00 per week, so if the Management do consider accepting the candidates, the father should be made to pay toward their keep.

27th November 1948. Barnardo's replied to the application:

We have read the report you have submitted in respect of this family of motherless children and feel that some help is indicated. We have it in mind to offer admission to June, Albert, Ethel, Douglas and Marion. Providing we are furnished with satisfactory Medical Certificates. Five Medical forms are enclosed and I should be obliged if you would arrange for these to be filled in and returned. If the admission of the five children mentioned is confirmed, we propose to ask the father to pay 10/- per week for each child, and this will include the Family Allowance in issue for them. In selecting the five youngest children for admission we have left Matthew and Thomas as companions for each other and Audrey and Olive likewise.

There was further correspondence concerning the completion of the medical reports because some incorrect dates of birth had been submitted. There was also difficulty finding an orphanage that could cope with the intake of all five children and concerns about the location.

When the paperwork was finally in order, an admittance date was arranged.

On 8th January 1949 the five youngest Thompson children were admitted to the Barnardo's Orphanage, Comlongon Castle. Dumfries, Scotland.

This must have been an extremely stressful time for my dad and the family. My sister Olive, who was the fourth child born and was ten years old at the time, told me years later that she clearly remembered the day we left home, because she had been told she, too, would be sent to the orphanage with the rest of us. She'd had a very tearful day at school saying goodbye to her school friends, thinking she would never see them again. Then, on the day of our admittance was she told only the five youngest were going.

The Barnardo's admission report states:

All five children are reported to be of normal mentality and satisfactory health.

However a second, undated report, just weeks after my admittance states: Marion has been admitted to Hospital suffering from Dermatitis of the legs and hair loss due to Alopecia.

On 19th January 1950, just one year after our arrival at Comlongon Castle, a letter was sent to my father informing him that June and May had been transferred to Mount Royal Hexham, Albert was sent to Beaconsfield, Douglas and Marion to stay in Scotland.

At that time Mount Royal and Beaconsfield were single sex residence and only accepted children of school age.

Dad was pleased to hear my elder siblings were moving back to England, because he had requested that we be placed closer to the family home so he could visit us occasionally.

Grandma, Dad holding me, Aunty Kit and eldest brother Bob
visiting the five youngest Thompson children at
Comlongon Castle 1949

A 5th February 1951 report states: *Comlongon Castle to
close.*

A month later, just three weeks before my 4th birthday,
I was transferred to join my sisters at Mount Royal, and
Douglas joined Albert at Beaconsfield.

I only have one vague memory of myself at that first
orphanage.

I can see myself as a toddler, standing at the bottom of a
cot with arms outstretched into the centre of a large room,
flanked by several cots down both sides. All the cots appear
to have babies or toddlers in them.

A lady wearing a white apron and hat is walking down the
centre of the room carrying a cake lit with candles. Everyone

in the room is singing and seemed to be happy. I realise now that it must have been somebody's birthday but I have no idea if it was mine.

4

Mount Royal

Barnardo's took ownership of Mount Royal to use as an orphanage in 1949.

Thanks to someone else's research, I recently discovered that Mount Royal was originally called Summer Rods Ridge and was built during the 1800's as part of the huge Summer Rods farming estate. The first documentation of the property was found on a Poll record for the County of Northumberland dated June/July 1826 with William Wilson as the resident.

The house then appears to have had several changes of residents until the death of John Stokoe in 1890. The estate was then owned by the Lockhart family until the house now known as Mount Royal, was used by the Royal Navy during World War II.

When my two elder sisters were transferred to Mount Royal from Scotland during January 1950, there is a distinct possibility that they could have been among the first residents to live at the newly established Orphanage.

When I was transferred to Mount Royal in March 1951, there were only two houses within the grounds; the enormous main house and a second smaller house located at the rear of the main building. Officially named 'Kings Cottage,' we just called it 'The Cottage.'

Mount Royal was initially an all-girls residence until 1953 when it became normal practice for brothers and sisters to arrive together. It is my understanding that, after this time, whenever possible siblings lived together under the same roof. My notes reveal that my elder brother Albert eventually joined us in 1954. His arrival reunited my family's five youngest children after we had been separated in 1950.

During my research, I discovered that my Dad was delighted we were all finally living at Mount Royal, because he had fought long and hard for us to be kept together.

I'm not sure if it was because of the influx of boys but it became necessary during the late 1950's for a bungalow to be built, just inside the main gates. The bungalow housed five girls aged between fourteen and fifteen. The purpose of living there was to prepare us for leaving the orphanage and entering the big, unknown world beyond the boundary walls.

My perception today of life in the bungalow is that we were segregated from the main group of children in the other two houses, in an attempt to de-institutionalise us before we left the orphanage.

Sadly, during my time there, it appears that girls leaving school were destined to become mother's helps or housekeepers. Boys, however, had the opportunity to attend Barnardo's William Baker Technical School, in Goldings, London, when they were aged between thirteen and fourteen, where they were taught practical skills. My two brothers were lucky enough to go there, and were taught their lifelong skills as carpenters.

During the 1950's A female Superintendent or Matron as we called her. Who was rarely seen 'on the floor' but, seemed to spend a lot of her time in the office was in charge, while the Staff who were generally middle-aged ladies supervised the children. We were instructed to call staff members 'Miss' before their surnames. Although when a married couple arrived in 1960, younger females were recruited and protocol became more relaxed. We were allowed to call them Uncle Ken and Aunty Jo and also call the staff 'aunty' followed by their Christian name.

The cottage and bungalow were each managed by one member of staff. They each had a private bedroom but I think they shared our bathroom.

The Staff in the main house slept and spent their free time in private accommodation situated above our cloakroom area at the rear of the main house. The staff quarters were accessed by a separate set of stairs, which were out of bounds to the children.

My favourite member of staff was Aunty Mary, who was possibly at Mount Royal for the duration of my time there. She had a great rapport and affinity with children. Her final position was being in charge of the bungalow, which meant I got to spend my last couple of years with her. She often talked of going home to visit her family, but that could only have been once a month, because she seemed to be always on duty.

All staff members were very understanding and fun loving with the exception of one. Unfortunately this particular member of staff appeared to get a great deal of pleasure from being mean and enjoyed dishing out punishment.

Obviously, I remember her name, but in this book have chosen to call her Evil Edna. She would say 'so you will' or 'so you won't' after every sentence.

For example she would often say, 'You won't be getting any tea, so you won't' or, 'you'll go to bed now, so you will.' In what I now know to be an Irish accent.

Not at all amusing at the time, but thankfully my sister and I can laugh about the memories of her now.

We did live within a strict regime. There was a never ending list of 'don't do this' and 'don't do that.'

I accept there had to be some form of discipline and control over so many children. The penance to pay if we were caught being unkind to others or breaking any of the rules depended on the gravity of the crime and, more to the point, which member of staff was on duty at that particular time. The punishments varied from a quick clip round the ear, doing extra chores, cleaning the toilets or, being grounded from going into town on Saturday. All of which were just accepted as 'life.' The worst punishment was being 'publicly flogged.'

I remember the time I was flogged. I was just ten years old and on evening meal duty in the dining room. My task was to be in charge of the very large teapot, the kind used in catering. It stood about 10 inch tall with a secondary handle above the spout to assist with pouring and steadying the sheer weight of it. I collected the very full and heavy teapot from the hatch and my job was to make sure everyone had their first cup of tea before placing the teapot back into the hatch, so the cook waiting on the other side could refill it ready for those who might want a second cup. The dinner smelled so appetising and I was very hungry. I had only just managed to finally sit down and start my meal, which, was by this time was starting getting cold, when one of the older girls asked for another cup of tea.

I remember being annoyed at her request because she had nearly finished her meal and I'd only had a few mouthfuls of mine, but, as expected of me, I dutifully returned to the hatch and retrieved the heavy teapot.

Just as I started to tip the teapot, she placed her hand over the top of her cup and laughing, said 'I've changed my mind.' The full teapot was so heavy I couldn't react quickly enough to halt the pouring, consequently a drop of hot tea fell onto her hand. She let out an almighty screech!

Gasps filled the air, as she accused me of scalding her. I tried to explain it was an accident and that I had not intentionally scalded her. I couldn't understand why the staff would not listen when I tried to tell them my side of the story. That she had actually placed her hand on top of the cup as I started pouring the tea, and because the teapot was so heavy my reactions were slow and the accident could not be prevented.

Unfortunately, the outcome was she had very red fingers which had to be held under cold water to prevent them from blistering. I was sent to stand outside the dining room door to await my punishment. As the other children left the dining room, most just walked past and sat on the rug in the hallway because, it was forbidden for anyone to talk to the child waiting to be punished. Some of my friends dared to make discreet contact with me and squeeze my hand. Sadly, I had seen several children being punished this way before but it was usually boys who were caught being naughty or breaking the rules.

When everyone was accounted for, I was summoned by the staff member to join her at the front of the group. She ranted on about my behaviour telling everyone I had to suffer the consequences for being so wicked. I was then physically bent over and hit on the buttocks with the large wooden clothes brush which was kept on the shelf close to the playrooms.

I tried to be brave and not cry in front of my friends but it was a very painful and emotional experience. The feeling of being humiliated in front of others was devastating. When the 'flogging' was over, I had to stand there until all the children had dispersed before I could leave the area and go straight to bed. I was distraught at being portrayed as a wicked person and upset that nobody would listen to my version of what had happened. I was also upset that I had missed eating my dinner! Reliving the events of that day still makes me feel incensed at the injustice. Yes, Evil Edna was the instigator and perpetrator of such acts.

I don't recall the existence of any complaint procedures being in place at that time, not that anybody dared complain anyway, because, 'Evil Edna' was the best friend of the Superintendent.

Children were treated differently during the 1950's. It appeared to be acceptable for a teacher to hit a child's knuckles with a wooden ruler as they passed by the desk, or humiliate pupils by making them stand in front of the class and hit them using a leather strap or cane. I am certainly not condoning the way adults treated children then. I'm merely emphasising that is how it was, in those days.

Thankfully, from about 1960, when a new superintendent took over the running of Mount Royal, everything changed for the better, the atmosphere in the home certainly became noticeably more relaxed.

Although we still had to abide by the house rules and be courteous towards others, we no longer had to live in fear of such punishments.

5

Bedtime

There was only one bedtime for all age groups. Nobody objected or caused any fuss or bother, in reality no one dared. Routine and rules were in place to be adhered to. We soon learned to just do it or suffer the consequences.

When we heard the familiar ding-a-ling of that little brass wooden handled bell echoing through the hallway at 6-30pm, we knew what it meant. That sound never failed to generate a huge surge of giddiness as we dashed about tidying up, the younger girls putting dolls back into the pram, collecting the crayons and drawing books, while the older girls finished off their embroidery or line of knitting or closed the lid on the box of an unfinished jigsaw. Everything had to be returned to its correct storage space before we rushed upstairs.

Half a dozen ten to twelve year old boys, dashed down the corridor to their territory on the right of the stair head, an area strictly out of bounds to girls.

The girls entered their zone, giggling and running through the huge landing area, past the floor-to-ceiling fitted cupboards which stored all the bedding and clothes, until they reached the two dormitories situated either side of a shared bathroom.

The dorm on the right was where six or seven eight to eleven year old girls slept, while the left hand dorm, with the luxury of an adjoining door to the bathroom, housed five or six twelve to thirteen year olds.

What a commotion ensued, girls stripping off, strewing clothes everywhere, but not for long. There were, of course, strict rules to be followed before we could enter the bathroom. All clothes had to be neatly folded and placed on the chair next to our bed. We were taught how to fold clothes neatly at a very early age. It was just another 'house rule.' If you are capable of taking an item of clothing off, you are able to fold it yourself.

There was no dawdling. Bath times were operated within a strict time limit. A member of staff would fill the bath with about six inches of warm water.

The depth was measured by her dipping her hand in the bath to check the depth. Fifteen minutes was the given time for each group of children to be bathed.

Time was of the essence. The first group of girls knew it wouldn't be long before a staff member returned to pull the plug out.

There was no supervision. The single member of staff on duty also checked the boys. Imagine the noise and banter as the youngest group of girls queued up, wrapped in their multi coloured striped towels, waiting for their turn to jump in the bath for a quick wash. As instructed, we used our flannels to wash face and neck first, then under arms, working our way down the body to the legs. Sometimes, there were two of the younger girls in the bath together.

When the member of staff returned to pull the plug out, occasionally, the last girl was still washing herself. She would try to submerge in the last inch of water to rinse off the carbolic soap as the water was draining away. It was pointless pleading for more time. The bath was given a quick wipe and then would be refilled with that precise amount of water for the older group of girls still waiting for their turn.

Getting dried was quite a skill. Stepping out of the bath still dripping wet and getting the bath mat soaking wet was on the 'forbidden to do' list. You were taught to stand in the bath with a towel wrapped around your back, dry face, under arms and body, then, rest a foot on the side of the bath. Only when it was dried dare we place it on the bath mat.

After putting our towels and flannels on our correctly named hooks, we would run for our lives out of the freezing cold bathroom, into the dormitory and put on our long sleeved flannelette nightdresses. Once everyone in the dorm was ready, we headed downstairs to the small kitchen to queue for our nightcap. We did everything together as a group. We were taught to wait for, and help each other. There was a very strong bond between us with very few arguments or outbursts of jealousy. Everything we had belonged to everyone else, that's just how it was.

Our lovely, larger-than-life, jolly cook always prepared an enormous pan of cocoa before she left to go home at 6pm each day. She was a local farmer's wife and lived just up the road. A member of staff would stand by the Aga, ladle at the ready. We would grab a mug lined up on the table. Girls would stand in the queue first with the boys, dressed in their striped flannelette pyjamas, one pace behind.

The member of staff would stir the contents of the pan vigorously as we advanced towards her then she would nod her head when it was time for us to hand her the mug.

She was an expert at pouring. Not only did she never spill a drop of cocoa down the side of the mug, she never failed to give each child their fair share of skin. To this day, if I see skin, I relive the nightmare of having to swallow that disgusting, slimy stuff. I soon learned the best way to deal with it was to take a deep breath and drink it all down in one go.

Only when our mugs were empty could we place them into the soapy water in the sink for the older girls on kitchen duty to wash up. Still chatting to the boys, we headed upstairs. It was time to say a final goodnight as we headed toward our respective dorms.

The girls returned to the bathroom, to clean our teeth and use the toilet for the final time. We pushed and shoved as we tried to find a space at the two small wash basins to clean our teeth then queued up to use the single toilet. We knew 7-30pm was the deadline. Everyone was expected to be in bed by that time.

Kneeling by our beds we said our prayers, to thank the Lord for keeping a roof over our heads and for the food on our table, before we slipped into the cool cotton sheets, covered by two prickly army blankets, and into bed. Then we could have what staff thought was our last chatter, before the lights out member of staff arrived.

We would all lie there waiting, wondering if our 'not so favourite' member of staff was on lights out duty.

She was the robust middle-aged lady known by us, as 'Evil Edna.' Sure enough it was her again. She used to barge through the dormitory doorway and briskly ask, 'Said your prayers?' A chorus of 'Yes Miss,' would ring out.

'Right, well, you'd better get yourself off to sleep and no nonsense or you will find yourself standing out on the landing. So you will.' We'd snuggle down into bed, not daring to let her see us smiling at the way she always finished her sentences. As the door closed behind her, and we heard her footsteps fading down the length of the landing, the dorm erupted with muffled laughter.

Now it was time for our bedtime entertainment to begin. It was great fun taking turns to tell each other stories, sing and act out our own version of nursery rhymes or try to recognise which member of staff was being imitated.

My favourite act was 'Guess that tune'. One of the girls was able to play amazing tunes by placing a hand flat under her armpit, then rapidly bringing her arm up and down. The outrageous sounds she made caused an eruption of raucous laughter. We enjoyed the entertainment so much we were willing to take the risk of being caught and suffer the punishment for the offence.

We desperately tried to ensure the staff in the room below us could not hear the laughter filling the dormitory. But alas, we made so much noise moving about on the iron-framed, metal sprung beds. It was only a matter of time before the inevitable happened.

A member of staff would burst through the doorway. We'd dive under our bed covers. The dorm immediately fell silent with children pretending to be asleep, except of course, the girl still in full motion entertaining at that particular time.

Most members of staff would just say 'Come on girls, it's time to settle down now.' So, we would stop the entertainment and go to sleep. But, not if it was Evil Edna. She'd say 'If you want to be awake you can be, but it will be standing on the landing at the top of the stairs. So it will.' The child caught out of bed suffered the punishment of standing at the stair head until it was time for staff to go to their rooms, which was usually about 9-30pm.

Frequently two or three children were standing on the landing, one from each dorm. It was strictly no talking or looking at each other. We would stand there rigid and silent, with hands behind our backs just staring ahead. Yes, there were times I was caught entertaining, and had to endure the punishment. There was no luxury of wearing a dressing gown or slippers for the duration. We could be left standing there, freezing, for up to two hours, hoping a more compassionate member of staff would retire to their room early and rescue us by saying 'Off to bed, and go to sleep.'

6

School Mornings

A typical school day began at 7am, with a member of staff barging through the dormitory door, switching the light on. "Good morning girls," she would say in a loud voice as she strolled down the centre of the room, pulling the bedding off each bed, leaving us lying uncovered as she moved toward the large bay window.

She would pull back the curtains and open the two side windows to their maximum, regardless of the weather conditions, causing a surge of cold air to fill the dorm. On winter mornings we saw evidence that Jack Frost had been out and about during the night, making beautiful patterns inside and outside the windowpanes.

Each morning the staff member would run a bath with the standard amount of warm water so anyone who had wet their bed overnight could get a quick dip. At least one of us had a wet bed every day. As an occasional bed wetter myself up to the age of seven, I can say none of the staff, other than 'Evil Edna,' created a fuss about who was wet.

As our beds had been stripped by staff anyway, it was just a matter of taking the bottom sheet off, wiping the plastic covering on the mattress with a dry part of the sheet, and then placing it in the wicker laundry basket standing just outside the door. The clean sheets were stored in one of the large cupboards on the landing. If I needed to get a quick dip, my sister or a friend would get a clean sheet for me. Only the children with wet beds were allowed a quick bath in the morning, so, as it was an open plan bathroom all the other girls could see who had wet the bed.

There was no such thing as privacy in those early days, but eventually, the bathroom was partitioned, making toilet and bathing areas private.

The children not bathing would be queuing, dancing and wriggling in desperation as they waited to use the single toilet. The relief of using the toilet was followed by the hustle and bustle of children trying to squeeze together to clean their teeth and get a quick lick with the facecloth at the two small washbasins available for all the girls. There was a general consensus that one basin was used for getting washed, and the other, for cleaning teeth, but that rule was often broken.

Before we left the bathroom, tooth brushes had to be placed back into our coloured plastic beakers with our individual little round tins of Gibbs foul tasting toothpaste positioned in front, within the correct allocated space on the shelving provided, and the stripy towels and face clothes hung back onto our personally named hooks.

Once back in the dorm we quickly dressed into our school uniform that we had neatly folded and placed on a bedside chair the night before. There were no mirrors to check if our uniform looked neat and tidy. We relied on each other, to make sure we looked smart.

Our beds had to be made in a very precise way. There were no fitted sheets in those days, so the flat bottom sheet was pulled straight then the surplus was tucked flat under the mattress. All the bedding corners had to be folded into the shape of a triangle, known then as hospital corners. The top sheet was placed over the top of the pillow just reaching the metal framework of the bed head, while at the bottom of the bed, the excess was tucked under the mattress. Next the two rough army blankets were positioned in line with the top sheet.

The tricky part was getting all the bedding positioned totally flat under the very thin lumpy mattress, making sure none of the bedding got snagged on the metal sprung base. The top sheet and blankets were then folded down flat, in line with the base of the pillow. We then slipped our neatly folded nightdresses under the pillow and threw the pale green counterpane over the top, with equal amounts hanging down both sides, finally making sure the surplus at the bottom was lying flat under the mattress. Not forgetting the hospital corners! Everyone helped each other, to make sure the beds were made correctly. After an anxious look around to check each bed space was tidy and we were suitably dressed, we stood by our beds ready for inspection.

Not a word was spoken as the Staff member looked at the beds to her left as she strolled down the centre of the dorm. Then she looked to the right as she headed back to the door. If all was well she would just walk on to the next bed, but if the bed making didn't meet the standard required, all the bedding was stripped off again. We soon learned to make our beds correctly the first time.

Inspection over, it was time for the morning cleaning duties to be done. The dormitories only got a quick sweep under the beds with a soft broom to collect the fluff. Imagine what state that bathroom was left in after the morning rush. The bathroom monitors gave the washbasins, bath and toilet, a quick wipe and mopped the floor. Upstairs duties were to be completed before breakfast.

Meanwhile, the children on dining room duty were already downstairs, checking the tables were correctly prepared for breakfast.

During my early years, the tables were set out with silverware, a butter dish and small butter knife, and toast was placed into a silver toast rack. A crystal dish with a silver lid had a quantity of marmalade in it. Milk and sugar were also presented in crystal glassware. Tea was always poured into a cup and saucer. Mugs were only to be used at suppertime.

We sat at small square tables with four chairs. Two tables were pushed together so the two members of staff could supervise the youngest children.

A little brass hand bell on the table in the hallway was rung to indicate breakfast was ready. Once we had entered the dining room we stood quietly behind our chairs until we were given the nod to sing grace in unison.

'Thank you for the world so sweet. Thank you for the food we eat.
Thank you for the birds that sing. Thank you God, for everything.'

Once we were seated there was no asking to be excused to use the toilet: It simply wasn't allowed to get out of our chairs until the meal was over, unless you were on dining room duty, handing the meals out as they were being passed through the hatch by the cook, or the child on tea pouring duty.

Without a doubt we were always offered a substantial breakfast.

In the winter months we started with a bowl of the cook's special thick, stodgy porridge. She soaked the oats overnight in a pan of cold water with a pinch of salt. Then in the morning the pan would be brought to the boil and left to simmer for a while before it was dished up. It looked like a dollop of thick glue on the plate, but once milk and sugar were added it was delicious. That was followed by a cooked meal, usually scrambled egg or beans on toast.

We were only excused to leave the dining room when staff had checked that everyone had finished their meal and there was no food wasted. The children on clearing tables passed the dishes back through the hatch to the children on washing up duty. One child to wash the dishes, one to dry and another to put the dishes back into the cupboards, before they could leave for school. Only senior children were allocated morning washing up duties because occasionally they were late finishing their chores and had to run all the way to Hexham so they wouldn't be late for school. Everyone else headed straight to the cloakroom to make sure they used the toilet and washed their hands before getting ready to leave by 8:15am.

The Junior and Senior schools were located in Hexham, a one and a half mile walk. Everyone was expected to be suitably dressed for the weather conditions of the day, for example, wearing wellingtons if it was raining. The senior children supervised the junior school children to the park gates, then, continued their journey an extra half mile to the secondary school. A member of staff always escorted and collected the children attending Lowgate Infants School, not quite a mile away.

There was a bus passing the gate on its way to Hexham each morning, but we were not allowed to travel on it. We were told it was only a bus for adults travelling to work between Allendale and Hexham. There was no alternative means of transport so the children of all age groups had to walk to school.

7

Infant School

During the 1950's, school terms began at the beginning of September, after the Christmas holidays, or after the Easter holidays. Children usually started school at the beginning of the new term in which they would celebrate their fifth birthday. My records show that I started school 03/09/1951.

A typical school day started by our following the usual morning routine of getting up and having breakfast. Then we'd have to wait until the mayhem of older children abated, while they were hastily getting ready to run or briskly walk into Hexham.

When all was quiet, we knew it was safe for us to head towards the cloakroom area, to use the toilet, change into our school shoes and navy Burberrys, collect our sandshoe bags, then line up to be inspected by the member of staff on escort duty. She checked we had everything we needed, and that we were suitably dressed for the weather on any given day. The inspection always ended with a questioning 'Have you been?' We never dared to reply no.

Infant school was just under a mile away from the orphanage. That was a very long way to walk at four years old, but I soon forgot about the distance because there were so many distractions on the way.

Our first place of interest was at the brow of the hill by the entrance to a farm. There was a purpose-built stone wall with a shelf that had at least six milk churns on. Some mornings, we would see the Elliott's milk lorry arriving to collect them. The driver would lift the heavy churns and place them onto the back of his lorry and replace the full churns with empty ones.

We were given permission to ask the driver where he was taking the full milk churns. He told us they were going to the Dairy in Hexham where the milk was bottled and said the empty churns left on the shelf were for the farmer to use when the cows were milked for the second time, later in the day. If we were a little earlier than usual and missed seeing the driver, he would beep his horn and wave as he drove past us on his way to the next collection point.

Continuing our journey, we passed a second farmhouse built so close to the footpath we could touch the windows but of course we didn't dare.

In the farm yard there was an area where the cow manure was stored. The stench was horrendous. Some children nipped their noses and ran past the pong but some, especially the boys, said they loved the smell of farm pooh and took a deep breath through their noses as they passed by. I was among the group of children that nipped their noses.

When we finally arrived at the school gate, the member of staff just left us. She probably did say goodbye but I never heard her. I was usually in such a rush to get into the school yard to play with my new-found friends before the school bell rang.

The pupils attending the Infant School were from the few local houses, and children who lived on one of the many remote farms in the area, and of course us kids from the orphanage.

The Infant School was an L-shaped building painted white with the window frames painted grey. There was a small kitchen area attached to the side of the main building where the dinner was delivered in containers from one of the larger schools in Hexham, just before lunchtime. At the rear of the building there was a veranda shielding the doorway to the open plan cloakroom area used by the children from both classrooms.

A second doorway led to the Hall which was used as the dining room and as a gym on rainy days. The last door sheltered by the veranda was for the communal toilets.

Schooling was so different compared to today, especially at our little country Infants school. There were only two classrooms for all the age groups, so we stayed in the same class with the same teacher for two years.

In the first class we sat at single desks in five rows with four desks in each, the youngest pupils sitting in the front row directly in front of the teacher and the blackboard, the rows continuing back in age groups until the eldest children sat in the row right at the back of the class.

Before class began we would stand at our desks until the teacher said, 'Good morning children.' Then we would chant, 'Good morning Mrs Capes.' She was a lovely, cheerful lady. I do not recall ever hearing a cross word from her. She used to take us out of school on nature walks and attempt to teach us the names of wild flowers, different types of grass and to name every tree and hedgerow growing in the area. We also knew the name of every wild bird there and recognised their calls.

We did of course have proper lessons, like Reading, Writing, Geography, History and Maths. Most of my lessons were enjoyable, but I do remember having difficulty with being a slow reader. I recall reading those Janet and John books for what seemed like forever, while other children moved on to other books. I finally managed to move on to another series of books by the time I left for junior school.

If I close my eyes and concentrate, I can picture myself sitting at my desk, the desk and seat was all in one, connected by a black iron framework. They were made with very dark brown wood and had a groove along the top to place your pencil or pen in and a hole with a removable glass inkwell.

Under the lid of the desk there was a deep box, with all the books we required for every lesson. So when the teacher announced the next lesson would be History, everyone already had the text book and exercise book.

I can still visualise the classroom walls decorated with brightly coloured posters. There were wall-charts displaying the two times up to twelve times table, beautiful wild flowers, British birds and the alphabet, to assist us during our lessons. We sang our tables in unison at the beginning of every Maths lesson. It didn't matter if we already knew the tables, we just sang them anyway.

My biggest problem at school was the toilets because they didn't have toilet rolls in them as they do today. If we wanted to use the toilet during lessons or playtime, we had to ask the teacher if we could have some toilet paper. You were only allowed one piece of crinkly Izal toilet paper if you wanted a wee but could have two if you needed a pooh. I did not find it easy to discreetly ask the teacher for toilet paper. I remember feeling embarrassed and I hated having to put my hand up and say. 'Please Miss, can I have some toilet paper?' knowing that she in turn would ask,

'How many pieces do you want, one, or two?' I often waited until I could barely walk to the toilet before I approached the teacher to be excused. It was so obvious I was desperate the teacher would just look at me and ask, 'one or two?'

Entering the only doorway to the toilet block and turning to the left, you saw four partitioned toilets for the girls and, to the right, a few steps past a central dividing wall to urinals for the boys.

I was not aware of any rules about the use of these mixed gender toilets and I never saw a sign indicating the direction for Boys or Girls. We just used them whenever necessary. I can only presume the boys used a partitioned toilet if they needed to sit down. The four washbasins fitted onto the back wall and the roller towel was used by everyone. I'm not sure if the teaching staff had their own toilet facilities or if they used ours.

Class two was for the seven to eight year olds, taught by Mr Nixon the Headmaster. He was a very nice teacher who spoke with a quiet voice.

In class two, we learned how to write with one of those very sharp pointy ink pens. Each morning, the class ink monitor removed the little glass container from each desk and part filled it with ink before placing it back into the hole. When we were introduced to an ink pen for the first time we were lectured about using it sensibly.

'Don't point the pen towards other pupils. It is not a weapon or toy.'

'Don't press down on the nib too hard while writing, that makes the nib buckle.

'Don't place the nib too far into the inkwell causing ink to drip before you write.'

Once the lecture was over we were given a pen, which was to last for the whole term.

I found writing with an ink pen very difficult at first, because I had previously only used a pencil. It took me a while to master the skill of not pressing down on the paper too hard, because that made the nib buckle slightly. Fortunately, the headmaster kept a box of replacement nibs on his desk, although it was a bit scary having to explain why you needed a new one.

There were quite a few mishaps in the early days, with pupils moving their hand across the writing before the ink had dried, causing the words to smudge.

We were each given a piece of blotting paper which was only supposed to be used before turning the page in your book. When it was time to leave for Junior School, we were nearly experts.

Also in class two, we still went out on nature walks. Sometimes we would sit at the edge of a field watching a Combine Harvester at work. I found it fascinating to watch the machine scoop up hay from the ground and then an oblong bale falling out the back. When we returned to the classroom, our great outdoor adventure turned into Art and Geography lessons as we tried to draw farm machinery and learn about the different crops grown in the area.

Just before lunch, the headmaster and a couple of the older boys in his class would assemble the tables and place a bench on either side ready for lunch. There didn't seem to be a caretaker available to help.

When the lunch bell rang, class was dismissed and we all scrambled to the toilet block to wash our hands then we rushed to line up at the serving hatch in the hall. There was only one lunch sitting. The youngest pupils were ushered to the front with the older children queuing behind. The kitchen lady would dish out a suitable portion of lunch directly from the containers onto a pale green plastic plate. We collected cutlery from a little side table and made our way to the dining table.

There was no choice of meal back then, just the meal of the day. We were always served basic meals, such as mince with potatoes and vegetables or shepherd's pie just on its own, sausage and mash or sausage casserole. We also had macaroni cheese or seasonal pumpkin pie.

Pudding was delicious; rice pudding with sultanas in. Semolina with a dollop of jam in the middle, we used to stir it up until the Semolina turned pink. We were also given Tapioca or frog spawn as we called it, Jam roly-poly with not-so-nice custard. During the summer term puddings were usually tinned fruit and jelly. Mr Nixon and Mrs Capes ate their meal once all the children were served. There was no lunchtime assistant on duty. Mrs Capes supervised the queue and doubled up as a dinner lady, by giving assistance to anyone unable to carry their plate, settle onto the bench or cut up their meat.

Everyone had to wait for the last person at the table to finish eating before we could clear the table. When we had all finished, we would take our plates back to the table, put our cutlery into a small bucket and stack our plates. Wasting food was frowned upon so there was very little waste.

During playtime breaks we were restricted to playing in the school yard, skipping, playing statues or hop scotch but, at lunchtimes, pupils could play more boisterous games on the school field. Basically, that meant the boys and some of the girls were free to run and play without fear of knocking any of the younger children over.

Not having a dinner lady meant there was no supervision in the yard or the field. I'm sure we were watched from a distance. We just enjoyed happily playing and if anyone fell over the Headmaster or teacher dealt with it.

Our daily PE lessons were very rarely held indoors. Whenever possible, we were outside. We didn't have a changing room or change into shorts and tee shirts, like pupils of today. In fact we just stripped off down to our knickers or underpants and vests in the communal cloakroom.

It was very fashionable to wear those thick navy blue baggy bloomers with elastic in the waist and legs. The boy's underpants looked much the same. I wasn't aware of any embarrassment.

During the lessons, we would throw bean bags into the air and catch them. Sometimes, bean bags were placed in a line on the opposite side of the school yard, for us to run back and forward collecting them one at a time, throwing them back into the box.

At times we would place a bean bag on our head, then stand on one leg and try to balance, balancing on our right leg first then the other. Not an easy task for some young children. Initially we were allowed to stick our arms out to help us balance but eventually we had to balance on one leg with arms by our sides. It was great fun, with lots of giggling going on. We also did skipping and running around the school field.At the end of the school day, the pupils from both classes would gather in the multi-purpose school hall, which was about the same size as the classrooms.

While the room was being used for Assembly, the wooden benches used at lunchtimes, and for PE lessons on a wet day were neatly stacked along the back wall alongside the foldaway tables.

In assembly, Mr Nixon would chat about the events of the day and tell us how good we had been then we all sang the hymn. *'Now the day is over, night is drawing nigh.'* When the singing was finished both Mr Nixon and Mrs Capes would say 'Good evening children' followed by a resounding chorus of 'Good evening Mr Nixon,' 'Good evening Mrs Capes.'

Then we dashed to the cloakroom area to get prepared for the walk home. Some parents collected their children by horse and cart or even by tractor, others walked home on their own. We, of course, had to wait at the gate for the staff to escort us back to the home.

8

Mams and Dads

I clearly remember one particular afternoon, while playing in the school yard, when I realised for the first time that my life was different to that of my school friends. It became apparent to me that the other children at school lived at home with parents and brothers or sisters. They had wanted to play Mams and Dads. I had not played that before. Of course, I knew I had siblings but this was the first time I had heard the words 'Mam and Dad.'

I found it difficult to concentrate on lessons for the rest of that afternoon. My mind was confused as I tried to understand how my classmates could live in a totally different environment. There were no Mams and Dads living at the orphanage. Why did I not realise that before now? I kept asking myself the same questions over and over. If everyone in school had a Mam and Dad, where were mine? Why didn't I have parents? Who could I ask?

We were not allowed to ask questions. What would I ask anyway?

As a child, I soon became aware children in the orphanage were discouraged from asking questions. If I asked Evil Edna a question, she always used to say. 'Ask no questions. Get no lies.'

I was so pleased when the school day was finally over. While walking home from school with the member of staff, I just blurted it out.

'What's a Mam and Dad? And, why haven't I got them?'

There was no immediate answer as she stared at me, then eventually she replied. 'I don't know. You might be able to find out when we get back home.'

When we arrived back at the orphanage, we were left in the cloakroom to follow the routine of hanging up our coats and changing out of our school shoes into our pumps then run upstairs to change into playing-out gear.

I have no idea of the time lapse, but I was eventually summoned to the office. The Superintendent was sitting at her desk and asked me why I had asked those questions. Quaking with fear and on the verge of crying, thinking I was in trouble for even daring to ask questions. I told her that the children at school had said they lived in a house with a Mam and Dad and, as I had not heard those words before I and wondered what they meant.

In a surprisingly gentle voice, she explained to me that I was living at Mount Royal because it was a Dr Barnardo Orphanage, where children who did not have parents to look after them lived and that I was now part of the Barnardo family. In reality, I didn't absorb everything she said but managed to pick up on key words.

My Mam had died when I was a baby and I did have a dad.

Despite not grasping every word, as always I just believed the words of an adult to be true, and I took her explanation on board without showing any emotion. At that moment, I did not consider there to be any reason why I should get upset or start crying. I was just so overwhelmed with excitement to hear that I did have a dad. Although I had no idea who he was, what he looked like, or where he lived, I was just so happy that I could now tell my friends that I had a dad too and it never entered my mind to ask anything about my mam.

The information given to me at that time seemed to satisfy my immediate curiosity. My understanding now, was that children not living at Mount Royal had a Mam and Dad. However, I didn't actually understand the concept or responsibility of what being a mother entailed, until I had my first child.

Reliving this moment, I find it upsetting I was oblivious to the consequences of not having a mother. I didn't think to ask how she died or what her name was. I also can't believe I waited until I was thirty years old before I found out her name was Olive. I have been told she had auburn hair but I've never seen a photo of her.

9

Lost Time

I was astonished to read in my Barnardo's archived records, that I had been absent from that country infant school from 09/02/1952 until 17/11/1952. The notes revealed I left Mount Royal to be boarded out, or fostered as it is known today.

9th February 1952:

Boarded out with a family in Durham.

4th March 1952:

Foster mother has written again. An early visit is absolutely necessary.

31st March.1952:

Letter from father requesting Marion's address he wishes to send her a birthday card.

18th April 1952:

Foster home not satisfactory a careful watch should be kept on Marion Thompson. There has been trouble with the little girl. Marion does not appear to be happy. Character Description: A quiet woe be-gone little girl.

Comment: *Although the Visitor has never seen her before, Marion was not frightened of the visitor, but has made no movement towards either foster mother or foster brother. There seems to be no life in her, such passivity is alarming in such a young child.*

15th July 1952: Assessment:

Both children are in the same bedroom again as Marion was lonely and a little frightened at night in a room by herself.

4th September 1952:

Father has written to ask us consider the restoration of girl. Father wants her back home.

Barnardo's Comments: Interested as to why he particularly picks Marion out of his five children. Thought this may be due to the fact that she is the only one boarded out. He has not seen her for three years.

2nd October 1952: Letter to father:

Thanking him for his note informing us that he only wishes to have Marion back in the home where he can visit once in a while instead of her being boarded out.

31st October 1952: Letter to father:

Stating there is a possibility of moving Marion back to Hexham, where it would be much easier for him to visit.

November 1952: Comment:

Foster mother not co-operative in matter of visits by father.

8th November 1952: Letter to father:

Informing him that we appreciate his feelings and that he will be pleased to know that Marion has been returned to Hexham.

I was really shocked when reading these notes for the first time. I found it difficult to believe the events were about me. Obviously, I don't recall my childhood on a day to day basis, but I find it weird that I have absolutely no recollection of the foster family I stayed with or anything about the school I attended during that time.

I can only imagine the experience of being whisked away from my siblings just a few weeks before my 5th birthday and being abandoned into what must have been a totally alien environment was so traumatic for me that I have obliterated it from my memory.

Initially, I asked myself what had taken so long to remove me from what appears to me to be an unsuitable situation. When clearly only one month into my placement, there were signs all was not well. With the first recorded visit in March, comments state, *'An early visit is absolutely necessary.'* Yet I was not returned to the orphanage until November.

Reflecting on the situation now, I realise all correspondence was hand written and, sent by post. Communication must have been a very slow process during 1952. The wizardry of computer technology was not prevalent in offices. So field workers did not have the luxury of sending documents and messages by email, as we do today.

My experience of being 'boarded out' is not a criticism of fostering care today. I have many friends who have successfully fostered or adopted children. I acknowledge fostering is a preferable alternative to children being in 'Homes.'

I am very grateful to the Barnardo's visitor (Case worker) who recognised I was in a precarious situation, unhappy and, needed to be rescued.

Although I didn't know my father at that time, it was reassuring for me to read that he had wanted me to be returned to my family.

I have a vivid recollection of a time I arrived at Mount Royal and seeing my sisters frantically waving and rushing forward to greet me, as I arrive in a car with wooden panels on the framework. That treasured memory of our joyful reunion will always stay with me.

My final comment on my experience; it appears to me, I had a lucky escape.

10

Junior School

I have no recollection of my first day at junior school, although I do remember a member of house staff escorted all new starting juniors to school each morning for their first week of term. I particularly remember that because I wanted to keep up with the elder junior pupils as we walked the one and a half miles into Hexham, but I was not allowed to, because all the new starters had to stay together and walk at the pace of the slowest child. It soon became apparent the older children wanted to keep their distance from us, so they would not be forced to walk in formation with us. I was so pleased when that first escort week was over.

There were two very distinctive groups of children heading towards the Hexham schools, the 'dawdlers' and the 'runners.' I preferred not to walk with the dawdlers because, I enjoyed a little play in the park before school time, so I attached myself to the runners.

Junior school was a large stone building with separate entrances for the boys and the girls. Once inside the two huge, black wrought-iron gates at the entrance for the girls, turning to the right, there were several steep steps leading to double doors painted bottle green. Passing through the doors, to the left there was the girls' cloakroom area and a wooden stairway leading to the Headmaster's office and the staffroom.

Then, through a second set of double doors, there was a very long walkway with classrooms on the left and windows stretching the full length of the corridor, which lead to the multi-purpose Hall which was used for assembly, as a dining room and for PE lessons. Outdoor PE was done in the school yard or on the park field, directly opposite the school.

I don't remember the names of any of the teachers, not even the headmaster's. However, I do recall this school was very different from my little infant school, because we had to change classroom for some of our lessons and quietly queue outside the door until the teacher beckoned us to enter.

I'm unable to remember much about the lessons, other than I still enjoyed my Geography, History and Maths lessons more than English. Because I became more aware that other pupils seemed to be better at reading and spelling than I was, and, I was always in trouble for the crossings out in my text book. It was also whilst at Juniors I realised I didn't know my right from my left. Eventually I mastered the problem by remembering, if I wrote with my right hand, the other, must be the left.

I enjoyed music lessons because I learned to read music and play the recorder. Imagine the noise as we all tried to learn Three Blind Mice and London's burning. We also did sight singing. That's when you sing the actual sound of the note on the music sheet rather than singing words to music.

Occasionally we travelled to the City Hall, Newcastle to participate in the annual Tynedale Schools Music Festival, where we competed against other pupils in the district. Our Junior School quite often won trophies for sight singing or singing in a choir.

When school finished there was always a member of staff waiting at the gate to escort us back to the home. Our route to the Allendale Road junction was determined by which member of staff was on duty. Most of the staff allowed us to play in the park until everyone was accounted for before we set off. We were allowed to let off steam by racing to the top of the hill where the towns' annual bonfire event took place. Then when we had reached the top, we shuffled into crocodile formation ready to walk along the alleyway leading to the main road.

There was never a doubt that up to ten children under the age of eleven needed to be supervised, but the rules about walking in public while being escorted were ambiguous.

The way we were assembled was determined by the interpretation of the rules by the individual member of staff. As long as we stayed on the footpath and stopped when we needed to cross the road, we could to skip or run ahead on our way up the hill back to the home.

I didn't like it when Evil Edna collected us though, because, she always had to show us she was in full control, by lining us up in 'crocodile formation' at the gates, then frog marching us back to the home.

My big sisters May and June wearing their Burberry coats.

11

Secondary School

For me, there was a great sense of achievement to finally attend secondary school. Those feelings were probably based on the fact I had spent at least eight years listening to the staff saying 'Little ones do this' and 'Seniors do that.' This lead me to imagine the senior children had a more exciting life than me but, in reality, being a senior only meant you were allocated more jobs and responsibility.

All children sent to the Secondary Modern School, as it was known then, went there because, like me, they had failed the 11 plus exam. Those who had passed the exam went to the Grammar School situated at the opposite side of the shared school field. I was only aware of one boy from the home going to the Grammar School during my time.

Both schools were located very close to the Mart on the east side of Hexham, which meant we had a trek of about two miles to get there. I remember one particular time when a new intake of children were not happy at the distance they had to walk to school and dared to ask why they couldn't catch the public transport bus passing our gates about 8:30am each morning.

Oh my! Evil Edna told them in no uncertain terms, that the bus was only used by working adults living in the

Allendale area or, from the surrounding isolated farms. If we boarded the bus there would be no seats for the public. It was not for the likes of us. An outcry of 'It's not fair!' filled the air. The new children continued protesting that the children from the posh houses of Southlands down the road from us were allowed on the bus, so why weren't they. Oh my goodness! It was very scary listening to these audacious children arguing about the rules. They soon learned though, that there was one member of staff you just didn't argue with.

I never dared to argue with staff. Living at the home so long meant that I had already become institutionalised and was a total conformist. Some days we had no alternative but to run to school, especially if we were on morning washing-up duty. Leaving the kitchen area before the last dish was put away would result in being given extra duties.

I enjoyed the freedom of running to school each day. Fortunately, it was downhill all the way until we reached the outskirts of Hexham, then we briskly walked through town and up the Eastgate bank, until we reached the little bridge giving us access to the school grounds.

The school was a cleverly-designed, red-brick, rectangular building with a veranda built around the inside of the structure, sheltering the entrances to all classrooms. There was beautiful lawn and rose garden in the centre of the quadrant. A purpose built hall with integrated gym equipment and a kitchen area were attached to the back of the main building.

The girl's toilets, cloakroom, and play areas were conveniently positioned at the opposite end of the building to the boy's facilities and yard. All the classrooms had windows along both outside walls, creating a light and airy environment for studying.

Several of my new-found friends at this school were curious about my parental status and asked me, 'What's it like not to have a mother?'

I just replied, 'What's it like to have one?'

Then we would continue chatting as if the question had never been asked.

Most of my lessons were enjoyable. Even my English comprehension was less stressful, despite my continued weakness with reading and spelling. I am convinced that during a spelling lesson I was the only pupil in class to be given a difficult word to spell, write it down twenty times and still get it wrong in a spelling test!

The lovely personality of the teacher made the lessons more enjoyable. She never made a public issue of any pupil's weakness. She just talked to them individually to reassure and help them overcome their problems. She certainly helped to boost my confidence with her kindness and understanding.

Learning a foreign language was a huge challenge for me. How on earth was I expected to cope with speaking French, when I had difficulty mastering English? I have absolutely no idea how or why I can still recite the French Verb, 'To Be' Je suis, tu es, il est, elle est, nous sommes, vous etes, ils sont, elles sont.

It's crazy that my brain has retained this information. Especially when I had no idea what the words meant, other than Je suis – I am. Recently a friend unravelled the mystery for me. I now understand the translation is; 'I am. You are. He is. She is. We are. You are. They are.'

Music lessons were great. We learned to recognise and name most classical music works and name the composers. I was in the school choir and enjoyed taking part in the annual Senior School Tynedale Music Festival, singing competitively against other school choirs at the City Hall in Newcastle. Occasionally, we returned with a treasured silver cup, kept in a trophy cabinet.

General Science lessons were both interesting and enjoyable topics. We were taught basic information about the human body, how electricity worked, and practical skills like changing an electrical plug. While the girls attended Domestic Science lessons, the boys did Woodwork and Technical Drawing. We learned Cooking, Knitting, Needlecraft, including darning socks using a wooden mushroom shaped object, and, of course, how to manage domestic chores and cleaning skills. Not that we needed any lessons on that topic!

During the autumn term, the new starters made their brown wrap around PE skirts. That was when I was introduced to the magnificent object called a treadle sewing machine. Learning how to use it for the first time was a terrifying experience because if I applied just the slightest pressure of my foot on the treadle, the mechanism of the machine set off at a rapid pace. It took an acquired skill to keep an eye on the needle, hold the material in place whilst also concentrating on the correct foot pressure.

By the time I left school, I had mastered making dresses, trousers and blouses for myself.

Those lessons were the foundation of my enthusiasm and love for dressmaking, which became my lifelong hobby.

I also loved the great outdoor life of PE lessons and enjoyed representing the school playing netball or rounders, I particularly enjoyed playing against other school teams. During the autumn and weather permitting, we played netball in the school yard and hockey on the school field but if the pitch was waterlogged or covered in snow, we switched to doing gym in the school hall. Gym entailed scaling the walls, nearly to the height of the ceiling, using a rope ladder and wooden framework attached to the walls. We vaulted over the horse, or balanced, while walking along an up turned bench. During spring term we played rounders and for the final term we did athletics.

I loved all the running events, especially the long distance races. Although running to school every day did give me an unfair advantage over the other pupils. My daily school run was also the foundation of my participation in several sponsored charity marathons and half marathon races as an adult.

Sadly, geography was no longer one of my favourite lessons when I moved to senior school. I had always enjoyed learning about the local environment and the names of the rivers and cities in England while I was at the infant and junior schools but, in my first year at seniors, everything changed. For the first time ever, I experienced a mean and vindictive teacher who seemed to get such pleasure from making an example of certain pupils and enjoyed embarrassing them in front of the class. Consequently, I felt overwhelmed with fear and trepidation whenever I knew geography was the next lesson.

I was fine when the teacher just talked about a particular topic and we had to make notes but when we were given our exercise books with a map of England showing unnamed rivers and cities, that was when panic set in.

There was a list of rivers and cities on the blackboard and our task was to write where they were located on the map. Although I could remember the names of most rivers and cities, I had a problem remembering where they were located on the map. So, while checking my work, if I had incorrectly named something, I would hastily cross out and rename. Therefore my work sheet ended up looking really messy. This particular teacher always made it quite clear that he did not like to be presented with untidy work in our exercise books.

I felt nauseous as we queued in the corridor waiting for the teacher to beckon us to enter. I could see a pile of books on his desk, ready to be distributed. Once we'd settled in our seats, he started to call out the names of pupils who then walked to the front of class to collect their books. The teacher would say 'Well done,' as he handed their books to them. My name always seemed to be among the last group to be shouted out. When I was finally called to collect my book, I was overwhelmed with fear as I walked to the front of class, because I just knew he would open my book and hold it up to show the rest of class my crossings out.

He would become very animated, go bright red and, almost jumping up and down and shout. 'You are an untidy camel, what are you?'

I then, had to repeat his words. 'I am an untidy camel Sir!' much to the amusement of everyone in the class.

There was one occasion when I was actually looking forward to the geography lesson, because the teacher had told us we were going to learn about a foreign country. When we arrived at the classroom door, we could see a huge map of the world hanging on the blackboard. Africa was the country he had chosen for us to study that day. The lesson was very interesting and I really enjoyed hearing about the people living in Africa. Naturally, I had seen a map of the world before that lesson and knew the names of many of the other countries but, until that lesson, I had no idea people living in another country had different coloured skin and talked a different language. In the pictures we were shown, all the people seemed to have bark-brown skin and tight, black, curly hair.

I put my hand up and asked the teacher; 'Why do people living in Africa have brown skin?'

He replied 'Africa is a very hot country and those people have a special pigmentation in their skin, to prevent the sun from burning them.'

I found this information confusing because at the orphanage there were two girls who had brown skin and tight black curly hair just like the people in those pictures. From that moment, I found it very difficult to concentrate, or listen to what he was saying for the remainder of the lesson.

Until that moment, it had never entered my mind that they might have come from another country, and I certainly didn't consider them to be any different to anyone else at the orphanage. There were children who had lily-white skin and orange hair, others who had almost white hair but we all played the same games and spoke the same language.

My head was overwhelmed by my own questions. If they were from Africa, how did they get to England? How did they know our language? We were learning how to speak French at school. Had they learned to speak English in their school before they arrived in Hexham?

I could not wait to get back to the home to ask the two girls my many questions.

At my first opportunity I asked one of the girls with brown skin where she was born. She looked surprised by my question, and replied 'London.'

I was so convinced she was from Africa, I had difficulty believing her reply.

'You can't have been born in London, because you have got brown skin.'

Continuing to explain how we had been shown pictures of people who live in Africa in our geography lesson and I told her that she looked just like them. She repeated her first reply saying, 'Well, I was told I was born in London.'

'How have you got brown skin then?' I asked

'Well your skin goes brown in the summer when the sun is out, does that mean you come from Africa?'

She had a valid point, I hadn't thought of that. I paused for a moment thinking of a reply. Then I blurted out,

'Yes, but only my face, arms and legs go brown, when they are exposed to the sun, but, in the winter months, my skin goes white again. Your skin is brown, all over.'

There were no raised voices or any unpleasantness between us. We were just calmly chatting about the topic while standing outside the cloakroom doorway, where the other children were continually running in and out.

I'm not sure if someone reported us, thinking we were arguing which was a punishable offence or if it was just a coincidence, but my favourite member of staff appeared and intervened, by asking if we needed any help with our discussion. I explained to her about the geography lesson and why I was questioning the girl.

Thankfully, this member of staff immediately understood my confusion and explained that some African people had travelled to England and, that there were African people living in some areas of England, particularly London. She also explained that if an African person had a baby while living in England, the baby would have brown skin just like the parent's. At last I understood that it was nothing to do with which country the girl was born in that made her brown, but her genetics. I was relieved that I was not considered to be a bully, just an inquisitive child asking why people had different coloured skin.

12

Ouch!!

Another memorable incident occurred while I was at the Secondary School.

After playing netball against a rival school the match had finished late. This meant I had missed the one and only bus to take me back to the orphanage. However I didn't have the slightest concern about the pending long trek uphill. I hastily gathered my things and set off.

It had been a very exciting day for me. Not only had we won the netball match but, I had also managed to shoot the last minute winning goal. And, during my home craft lesson earlier in the day, I had finally achieved a different goal. It was finally my turn to be shown how to knit mittens using a set of four needles. I'd had my eye on a ball of bright yellow wool in the knitting box for some time, and had watched anxiously during past lessons in case anyone else chose it before me. I longed for a pair of yellow mittens to match the beret I wore for church on Sundays.

Whilst slowly meandering through town with a smile on my face, I headed towards the road home. I realised it was imperative that I arrive home before tea time. Being late for any meal was not tolerated, no matter what excuse was given, so I increased my pace and headed home with my PE bag slung over my shoulder and my treasured knitting in hand. With no watch for guidance and no concept of time, I was sure I was going to be late for tea.

Slipping the knitting into my pocket, I started to run. Ouch!! After only a few strides I felt a sharp shooting pain in my right knee, which stopped me in my tracks. Looking down, to my horror I could see one of the knitting needles sticking out of my leg. The needle had pierced my leg, hit the bone and found its exit just to the right of my knee, the needle was now bent at an angle. I froze to the spot, unsure of what to do next. The warning I had heard numerous times before echoed in my head.

'Never put knitting needles in your pocket.'

I started to cry, not because my leg was hurting but for fear of what might happen to me for disobeying that rule. My mind was focused on thinking about the consequences of having a needle in my leg, and possibly, now being late for tea and, wondering which punishment I would have to endure. My knee was throbbing but surprisingly there was very little blood. I stood for a while, then, after inspecting the damage, I eased myself upright, then flexed my knee gently to see if it was working. Thankfully, it was.

Reaching into my pocket to retrieve my knitting, I was so pleased to find that I hadn't dropped any of the stitches from my precious yellow mittens. It was the loose needle that had caused the damage. I knew nobody would be around to come to my rescue. It was very rare for a car to pass by and no one, other than us kids from the home, ever walked up that road. So, with the needle still firmly in place I set off walking, or should I say limping, the final mile home. The time seemed to drag by as I limped my way homeward. The hill appeared to be far steeper than usual.

Then, in the distance, I spotted someone wearing a very distinctive navy blue Burberry. That sighting immediately lifted my spirit. It just had to be one of us kids from the home. We were instantly recognisable wherever we went. No one else in town had ever been seen wearing those coats.

I increased my pace, in an attempt to catch up with that Burberry. As I got closer, I could see it was one of the boys from the home. I was surprised when he told me that he had dared to spend the 2 pence given to him for his bus fare on sweets, and didn't seem to have a care in the world. He was so reassuring that we wouldn't be late for tea and being late was never a problem to him anyway. '

'What's the matter with you?' he asked 'have you fallen over?'

'No,' I replied, 'just had an accident with my knitting.'

He burst out laughing, 'Your knitting!'

'Yes,' I replied, and showed him my knee, which instantly silenced him and wiped the grin off his face. 'Oh my, how did you do that?'

After I explained the events to him, he took a closer look at the protruding needle and declared, 'That needs to come out.'

Then, before I had time to respond, he grabbed the needle and yanked it out.

'There you go,' he said, 'Done.'

I was so shocked I didn't have time to register the pain. With a cheeky smirk on his face, he handed me the bent needle. I was stunned, the needle was almost bent in half, yet, it had slipped out so easily, the extraction wasn't as painful as I had expected it to be, and, remarkably there was very little blood.

Without further ado, we increased our pace and continued the uphill journey, towards the home. Thankfully, when that incident happened I was living in the bungalow situated at the entrance of the main gates, quite a distance from the main house, with easy access without being seen by anyone in the main house. The bungalow housed five girls supervised by my favourite staff member. She was the most tolerant understanding person I had ever met.

On our arrival, we knew it must already be tea time because of the silence. Generally, before mealtime the grounds would be full of noise and laughter, while the children played.

'See you later' the boy shouted, as he set off running up the drive and disappeared around the bend.

I crept up to the outhouse, which was used as a cloakroom, and opened the door slowly. The door was renowned for having creaking hinges. What a relief. On this occasion the door opened quietly. Taking my coat off and changing into my indoor shoes, I stood for a while, thinking how would explain the situation I had found myself in. One of the children came looking for me.

'Hurry up' she said, we're about to start tea, I've been sent to look for you.'

'Just got back,' I replied, trying not to limp or show any emotion.

I entered the dining room and sat in my place and apologised for being late, without offering an excuse.

The events had left me feeling rather sick, but, despite not feeling the slightest bit hungry, I managed to eat all my meal as expected of me.

After the table was cleared and the girls were doing their house duties, I showed the member of staff my bent knitting needle and asked if she knew how to straighten it.

'My goodness, how did that happen?' she asked. Not daring to lie, I told her the whole story. She looked horrified when I showed her my leg. Expecting at the very least a good telling off, to my relief, she just said,

'Now you know why we tell you not to put knitting needles in your pocket.'

She wiped the puncture wounds with cotton wool soaked in stinging Iodine.

I have no idea how the needle was straightened, but I did finish my treasured mittens, and, learned my lesson. I never put needles in my pocket again!

13

Nitti Nora

Although I don't think the term 'Nitti Nora the head explorer,' was used during the 1950's, I have decided to use the phrase to replace the names of staff who carried out the Friday night head inspection duty.

This duty was done in various locations throughout the house. There was a time when our hair was inspected in the quiet playing room, but I particularly remember apprehensively queuing on the landing outside the bathroom. We could see her standing by the open window preparing the solutions.

A distinctive odour filled the air as she poured out the strong smelling lotion Zulio, known then, to be the exterminator of lice and nits into a small white enamel bowl. Another bowl had already been prepared with disinfectant and the fine metal-toothed comb and a roll of Izal toilet paper lay close by.

Once the preparations were done, 'Nitti Nora' gave the customary nod of her head, indicating she was ready for us to approach. Stepping forward, we grabbed our multi striped towel from the row of hooks and wrapped it round our shoulders. There was a tut of disapproval if we weren't quite ready as we reached her.

Having that metal comb dragged through the hair was very painful, as it was pressed into the scalp to make sure nothing escaped. It was particularly agonising when the hair was lifted and the comb dragged upwards as she hunted for nits hiding behind the ears, but none of us dared to squeal, because that would trigger a lecture on reasons why it was not advisable to have head lice and spread them to others. We knew from experience that it was best to comb our own hair to get rid of the tats before the procedure. Glancing at her face, I was never too sure, if that was a smirk or a grimace.

The 'Nit-Kit' came with a small metal strip which was used to scrape any debris collected in the comb onto a piece of crisp Izal toilet paper. All objects falling onto the paper were closely scrutinised and anything moving was firmly placed between the thumb nails and crushed. If this procedure caused a distinctive popping sound, then that was it confirmed. You definitely had nits. If just one creepy crawly was found, it was an immediate step toward to the second bowl, where a sponge was used to soak that freezing cold smelly Zulio stuff into the scalp. Oh boy did that stuff stink! There was no disguising you had nits. The solution was to be soaked into the hair for 24hrs.

We never felt alone though, plenty of other children had nits too. It was immediately obvious if someone got the all clear because they were the lucky ones with a grin on their faces as they walked straight past the second bowl and made their escape.

Of course, the experience of the procedure inevitably depended on which member of staff was doing 'Nitti Nora' duty. If 'Evil Edna' was on duty, she always appeared to relish a little extra tugging and pulling.

14

Saturdays

Living a life of strict routine meant my body clock woke me by 7am every day.

Any children who woke up before the official wake-up call were allowed to use the toilet but had to return to their beds until the member of staff on duty that morning granted us permission to get up. We happily entertained ourselves, by mimicking the different ways a member of staff would barge through the door with a jovial 'Good morning girls'. Poor Evil Edna always got the biggest laugh, because she was incapable of being happy.

Once the signal was given, we quickly dressed into our comfortable, well-worn hand-me-down playing out clothes. Saturday was the day we would actually look like little orphans.

As the morning was the designated time for the house being thoroughly cleaned upstairs and down, or 'bottomed' as it was called, the morning routine was slightly different. Our jobs started with us changing the bottom sheet of our beds.

So, as the member of staff had already very kindly pulled our bedding off as she headed down the centre of the dormitory to open the windows, we would grab the bottom sheet, crumple it up and throw it into the square wicker laundry basket on the landing, then collect a clean crisp sheet from the huge cupboard on the landing and return to make our beds.

The sheet used on the top last week now became the bottom sheet and the clean sheet went on top. We gave the two prickly army blankets a good shake before placing them back on the bed then finally neatly placed the candlewick bedspread over the top. Although I remember the bedspreads were laundered once a month, I have no recollection of when, or if, the two prickly army blankets got changed.

Once our beds were made and inspected, we set off downstairs to wait for the breakfast-bell to ring out. As always we were provided with a substantial breakfast starting with thick porridge with milk and a sprinkle of sugar on top during the winter months or cereal for starters in summer, followed by a crispy piece of bacon served with beans or scrambled egg on toast, and as always, toast and marmalade with a lovely cup of tea.

After being dismissed from the dining room, we would check our allocated jobs for the day on the duty roster pinned to the wall by the back door. All children over the age of seven were considered eligible to be given a task. The youngest ones did lightweight jobs like dusting. At least two children were assigned to do each job, usually one junior child and senior.

I considered myself to be very lucky because I was quite often paired up with either of my two elder sisters. For me that meant I was less likely to be bossed about too much.

Cleaners may have been employed during the hours we were at school, but I certainly didn't see any. Not even during the school holidays. It was my understanding that we were the only cleaners during the 1950's.

We did have a resident gardener in my early years though. He and his wife lived in a tiny cottage attached to the laundry room at the back of the main building. He was responsible for looking after the vast grounds which included a tennis court, pond and an orchard and a very large vegetable plot, while his wife supervised the laundry and ironing duties.

The general consensus then was that the girls did the indoor household chores while the boys did the outdoor jobs with guidance from the gardener. They weeded the gravelled driveway, the vegetable patch and kept the vast grounds tidy, chopped sticks for the fires, and helped to saw the logs.

There must have been exceptions to that ruling because this is a photo of myself standing in front of the log cutting.

It clearly shows girls doing log duty on that particular day.

My sister and her friend are sitting on top of the log to keep it steady while the two members of staff use an enormous dangerous-looking saw to cut the log.

I'm not sure this image would meet with today's Health and Safety guidelines!

Dormitory Duty: The girls were assigned to each dormitory. A child would stand at each end of the carpet runner, which ran the full length down the centre of the dorm. By using hand-held, firm-bristled, carpet brushes, they got down onto their knees and started sweeping as they went along, meeting in the centre. The carpet was then rolled and placed outside the door. Then, with a softer-bristled brush, the floor would be swept. Next, the skirting boards and underneath each bed, making sure they were free of dust and fluff. All debris was collected into a dustpan. The metal framework of the beds and the window sills were dusted with a yellow duster. Once all the cleaning duties were done, the runner carpet was returned to its precise position.

Bathroom Duty: The two girls on bathroom duty took turns to do the tasks set for them. One child would clean the two hand basins, making sure they were clear of toothpaste spit or tide marks, wiping down the front and sides of the basin, not forgetting the pedestal. The bath was also cleaned. Meanwhile, the other girl would wipe the small, white, wooden bookcase used to store all our tooth cleaning gear, then after all the paintwork had been wiped clean, the toothbrushes were put back into the beakers which were then put back onto the shelves, placed the precise distance apart, with all the brush heads facing the same way. The individual little round tins of that disgusting foul-tasting Gibbs toothpaste were positioned in front. A clean towel and face cloth, which was to be used for the next week, was hung on each named hook.

I hated cleaning the toilet, even after we were issued with a hand brush to remove the marks on the inner bowl and, squirmed when I had to wipe the wooden handle at the end of the system chain, because the chain was pulled before anyone washed their hands and in the early days we did not wear protective rubber gloves. After cleaning the toilet and washbasins, we washed the bathroom floor. The final upstairs job was to run a carpet sweeper over the landing carpet.

Driveway Duty: The chosen two children for this duty started at the main gate with a wheelbarrow, both of them armed with a long-handled hoe. Their task was to hoe their way up the long, curved driveway, removing all weeds peering through the gravel picking up any fallen debris or foliage from the surrounding trees, until they reached the entrance of the main building. Once that job was done, they returned to the main gate with rakes to smooth out the gravel over the tyre tracks. Although family visitors were very scarce, the driveway only looked smooth for a few days until a bus load of ladies from one of the regional WI's would flatten the gravel down again.

Gardening Duty: Under the watchful eye of the gardener, the boys weeded the vegetable patch and the flower gardens. Particular care was taken weeding the beautiful rose garden situated in front of the main building. The lawns always looked neat and tidy, yet I have absolutely no recollection of how they were kept so trim. Maybe a push along mower was used or possibly a petrol lawnmower?

The boys seemed relieved the gardener was in charge of inspecting their duties, because he was a cheerful character with a very mild mannered temperament. I remember the gardener and his wife being around for many years. I wonder who helped him with his duties before boys came to live at the orphanage?

Shoe Cleaning Duty: A shoe-cleaning box was kept in the cloakroom at all times so shoes could be cleaned on a daily basis if necessary. The box had three partitions. Each section had two bristle hand brushes clearly labelled polish-on or shine, accompanied by little round tins of Cherry Shoe Polish, Black, Brown and Tan.

During the winter months, all shoes were either Black or Brown. Tan sandals were generally worn between Easter and the September term.

One child would work their way along the row of cubby holes where our shoes were stored, making sure the brush labelled 'polish-on' was used to sparingly rub polish from the little round tins onto the shoes. Only one dip of the brush into the tin of polish for each pair of shoes was allowed. The second child followed closely behind, buffing off the polish with the 'shine brush.' Obviously it was easier, and less likely to cause a mishap, if all the shoes of the same colour were cleaned in one go.

Woe-betide if anyone got the brushes or polishes mixed up! Inevitably, there were occasional mishaps when tan shoes were accidently cleaned with black or brown polish, causing great upset and a good ear bashing for the offender.

Any shoes with holes in the soles or the heels worn down were polished then put to one side for further scrutiny by a member of staff. She would decide if the shoes were beyond repair or if the gardener could mend them by using his last and tiny tacks to replace the sole or heel.

It was fascinating to watch him as he searched through his box of various-sized new soles and heels trying to find the nearest fit for the shoe and quite amusing when he accidently hit his fingers with the hammer as he tried to knock the tiny nails in!

Cloakroom Duty: While the shoes were being cleaned, two other children shared the job of washing the toilet and hand basin area and changing the roller towel. In the early days, it was not an easy task to do without the protection of rubber gloves or, the use of a toilet brush, to protect us against freezing cold water.

A member of staff prepared the metal-bucket with disinfectant water before we started. With a clean cloth, we wiped the taps first, then the washbasins and pedestals. After rinsing the cloth, it was time to wash the toilet doors inside and out, not forgetting to do the door handles.

We then precariously balanced with a foot on each side of the toilet bowl, as we wiped the high level cistern and run the cloth down the toilet chain and wooden handle. We gave the cloth another rinse before wiping both sides of the seat and the outside of the bowl.

Then, with eyes scrunched tightly shut, we would take a deep breath and plunge our hands into the freezing cold water, using the cloth to remove all the marks and stains from inside the bowl.

After checking all the porcelain was spotless, we swept then mopped the floor. An equal amount of the by now dirty disinfectant water was poured down each toilet and flushed away. The final job was to replace the dirty multi striped roller towel, which had been used to dry the hands of at least twenty children on numerous occasions during the previous week.

Silver Cleaning Duty: The cutlery we used on a daily basis was real silver and had to be cleaned every Saturday. There were no special magic cloths for cleaning silverware in those days. The two girls allocated the duty would place all the cutlery and silverware into the centre of the kitchen table which had been covered with old newspapers.

There were so many pieces to clean. Bone handled dinner and dessert knives, butter knives, forks, dessert spoons, soup spoons, tea spoons, serving spoons not forgetting the toast racks and companion sets. Each girl wrapped a part of the duster around their index finger and dipped into the cream coloured liquid Silvo polish, with the distinctive smell filling the air and stinging our noses. Methodically and sparingly, we smoothed polish over every item. That job done, we used a clean part of the duster to vigorously rub all the polish off again.

Once all items looked clean and shiny again, everything was then submerged into hot soapy water and left to soak while the dirty sheets of newspaper would be rolled up and tied into a knot, making paper sticks for lighting the open fires. The same two girls washed and dried everything, then used a dry tea towel to give a final shine, before putting the cutlery and other silver items away into the drawers or cupboard. We soon learned it made sense to keep the cutlery in groups, knives, forks and spoons etc. That made life much easier when it came to putting everything away.

Finally, after putting the polish away we took the dirty dusters to the laundry room. I hated silver duty, the strong smell hurt my nose and the process made my hands filthy.

Ballroom Duty: Very few children disliked Ballroom duty. It was hard work but it could also create so much fun and laughter. The parquet flooring in the huge room had to be swept and polished and window sills and skirting boards dusted. The youngest girl would start the process by dusting the windowsills and skirting boards while the boys assisted with the removal of furniture. We stacked the chairs and the boys placed them in the small passageway outside the door. If the table tennis equipment had been in use the previous evening, it had to be folded in half before it would pass through the doorway. Not an easy task.

The table had to be tipped onto its side, so the trestle legs could be unbolted and folded inwards before the table top was folded in half. The two halves were secured together with a little hook and nail on each side. Then, by tipping it backwards and forwards a few times, ensuring we didn't trap any fingers in the process, the girls wedged a couple of dusters underneath to enable the huge object to slide outside the door without damaging the beautiful flooring.

We laughed so much when we had near misses, as the structure threatened to fall on top of us! Once the furniture was moved the boys disappeared. Sweeping and polishing the floor was considered to be girls or women's work.

We started by brushing the floor with a soft brush and collecting all the debris in a hand-held dustpan. Then, using a clean cloth which was usually an old vest or garment, two girls on hands and knees side by side would sparingly rub wood polish onto the parquet blocks. Starting at the back wall inch by inch, we worked our way backwards towards the door. We rubbed back and forth, moving to the beat of the songs we sang.

The final task was to bumper the polish off. The bumper was a solid, heavy, oblong structure, roughly the size of a breeze block today. It had a long, wooden, broom-type handle attached to the centre by a double hinge. A piece of sheepskin cloth with elastic edges was slipped under the base.

Then the part we loved the most. With both girls hanging onto the long handle, the heavy bumper was thrust into the distance and pulled back again. This action was repeated until all the polish was buffered off. Occasionally, the sheer weight of the bumper would drag a skinny little runt like me along the floor behind it, which was a very frightening experience the first time it happened, but, eventually we found it so much fun, which created uncontrollable laughter.

The stairs, hallway, playrooms and the dining room were all on the 'to be cleaned' list. All chores had to be completed before the lunchtime bell rang out. There was not an idle child in sight on Saturday mornings, although some children managed to master the skill of pretending they were being industrious even if they were messing about.

It was an acquired skill to make any given job last just long enough, so there was no time to start another one before lunch. I'm sure the staff were onto that ploy though.

After such a busy morning, we were really ready for our appetising lunch of a sausage casserole or shepherd's pie, with vegetables, followed by jam roly-poly accompanied by the usual horrid lumpy custard. When the dishes were washed and everything was put away, the children who wanted to go into town queued outside the office door for their pocket money but only after changing out of their playing out clothes into smart outfits.

Pocket Money: Junior children were given three big round copper coloured one penny pieces, or a hexagon shaped three-penny bit. The seniors got a shiny silver sixpence.

I remember queuing for pocket money, and having three big one penny pieces to buy sweets in town, but couldn't recall the details of how it was distributed.

My elder sister reminded me recently that there was a pocket money book to register the amount each child was entitled to, and that we had to save at least one penny every week. I remember having a Post Office savings book given to me when I was about eleven and being told not to spend all my money on sweets. We were trusted to go to the Post Office ourselves and put money into our account. That was my induction to being in control of my own finances. Well, what I mean is, at least I was responsible for my own pocket money savings.

Town Visits: Any child who attended the Junior or Senior schools in Hexham, who was not grounded by a misbehaviour order was allowed to walk into town without staff supervision. Obviously this did not mean total freedom to roam beyond the gates without guidance. The senior children aged between 13-15 years were responsible for the behaviour and welfare of the younger ones.

Being the youngest of five siblings meant that I always had someone to take me into town. It was usually one of my sisters who took me. I expect my brothers didn't want a little sister tagging along with them.

Once the junior children had convinced the member of staff they did have somebody to supervise them we were allowed to set off for our trip to town.

It never seemed to be important what time we set off for town, but it was imperative everyone had to report back by 4pm. By the time we walked the mile and a half each way into town, bought sweets and called into the Post Office the trip usually took us two hours.

On the way to town, we generally just followed the route we did every day on our school run. We would wave and shout hello to the affluent residents of 'Southlands,' a row of very smart houses where our Sunday school teacher lived. Then, passing a very large farm house, we clambered up onto the top of a stone wall to see the sheep and lambs we could hear, but not see, on the other side of the very high wall.

The footpath ran out just beside the driveway of an antique shop owner's very large house. There was a slight bend in the road which obscured the view of oncoming traffic, so we had to listen very carefully and watch for any traffic before crossing to the opposite path.

There were very few cars on the roads during the fifties, so it was extremely rare to see a passing motorist, and cars certainly did not travel at high speed. If anyone did pass us, they would sound their horn and wave. Everyone knew who we were, clad in our navy-blue Burberrys.

Once safely across the road, the pavement led us to the entrance of the Domestic Science, Teachers Training College, known as 'The Hydro,' where some of the students who kindly volunteered to teach us sewing and dancing lived.

Opposite this driveway was yet another huge house owned by an Ophthalmic Specialist. We knew his occupation by the writing on the brass plaque on his gate post. He always said hello or waved and smiled if we saw him in his garden.

We continued to pass large houses, until we eventually came to the last house situated at the junction where the Allendale road met the main route between Newcastle and Carlisle as it passed through Hexham. This enormous house was being used as the Fire Station and the British Red Cross Ambulance Station. (The senior children attended that building once a week to learn First Aid.)

We had to take extreme care to cross that fairly busy junction, where at least two or three cars passed within half an hour period. There were no traffic lights to assist with crossing the road then.

Once in town, we soon reached our favourite sweet shop Guthrie's. His shop window displayed hundreds of jars with tempting colourful sweets. For us, it was big decision time. Do we buy our sweets now? Or, do we venture further into town to check out Woolworths to see what was on offer there? My dilemma was that 'Woolies' often had special offers on their chocolate items which were tasty but didn't last as long as Guthrie's hard boiled sweets. With hindsight the decision was fairly straight forward.

Guthrie's sweets were the best value. So for me and my sister, Guthrie's it was.

Inside Guthrie's shop, a little bell above us rang out as we opened the door. He would appear from the rear of the shop wearing a beige overall, clasping his hands and greeting us with a smile. 'Hello girls, what would you like today?' (He was just like the Ronnie Barker character as seen on TV.)

With eyes wide open, we looked at the jars of sweets stacked on shelves and the boxes of goodies under the glass counter, wondering what to choose. There were pineapple cubes, pear drops, aniseeds balls, sherbet dips, Spangles, gobstoppers, Liquorice torpedoes, Liquorice Allsorts and Liquorice Root to name a few. Does anyone remember liquorice root? It looked like a piece of twig from a tree, and had a peculiar taste while being chewed. Looking back now, it was quite disgusting.

At Guthrie's shop, we could buy an ounce of one type of sweet or ask for a penny mix. There were no electronic weighing scales then. He would place a one ounce weight on one end of his brass scales then pour the sweets from the jar straight into the shiny bowl on the opposite side of the weight.

The scales started to waver if the weight went over. He would grab a handful of sweets out of the bowl and start dropping them back in, one at a time, until he decided the balance was correct. He was such a kindly soul, and would drop a few extras in before pouring the sweets into a little cone shaped paper bag he made himself by scrolling a flat piece of paper and bending the pointed end upwards to secure the end.

We happily handed over our one or two pennies and left the shop to the echo of his joyful voice saying, 'See you next week.'

I had never heard the term 'window shopping', while I lived at Mount Royal, so we didn't hang around looking in shop windows. We only looked at shops with sweets displayed in the window. Once we had bought our sweets and put our left over money in the Post Office it was time to head back to the orphanage.

We preferred to choose a different route for the walk back home, so we walked past the Allendale Road junction and headed in the direction of Carlisle until we came to a second junction on the left. This road cut through a street of terraced houses to a little country alleyway which ran behind the back of the Hydro College and stopped at the driveway of the local horse trainer and land owner. Once across the drive we entered one of his fields through what we called a 'Wishing gate' because we used to stop and make a wish every time we passed through it. It was a four foot tall structure of wrought iron in the shape of a half circle, with an iron post and a secure swing-gate facing the centre.

Basically, you stepped inside the gate, leaned against one side of the half circle, pushing the gate towards the centre of the circle you then manoeuvred behind the gate as it swung to the opposite side. This style of gate prevented animals grazing in the field from escaping. I have since learned the correct name for this type of gate is a 'Kissing Gate.' I can assure you there was certainly no kissing going on when we used that type of gate. After passing through several of these gates we reconnected with the main Allendale road for the final short walk back..

We always made sure we still had a few sweets left by the time we arrived back at the Orphanage, just in case the member of staff asked to see what had we spent our money on when we returned our saving book. It was a punishable offence to arrive back without having something to show for our money.

The punishments always depended on which member of staff was on duty and varied from doing extra chores, being forbidden to play out or even to miss our tea, if it was deemed we had been too greedy and eaten too many sweets. The latter of the punishments was a favourite of Evil Edna's.

Once tea was over, we could play out in the grounds until the large brass bell above the back door rang out, letting us know it was time to return to the house for bedtime.

Straight after our Saturday evening bath, was the designated day of the week for us to change our underwear. So, we would rummage for underwear on a shelf in the treasure trove cupboard on the landing to find clean knickers, vest and a liberty bodice during winter. Behind the first set of double doors there were rails of dresses, party dresses for all the Christmas parties we attended. Smart dresses or kilts were worn for our three trips to church on Sundays and there were outfits of smart clothes to be worn if we went into town on Saturday.

The shelf directly below the hanging rails was packed with school jumpers and blouses, with the bottom shelf for all the underwear, white cotton vests, cream liberty bodices with little rubber buttons and big, baggy navy-blue knickers with elastic in the waistband and legs. Some of them even had little pockets sewn on them.

Finding clean underwear to fit me could be tricky. I had to try several vests and knickers on before I found the most comfortable and best fit for me because they had to last me for a whole week. Being such a skinny kid, I always had a problem finding a pair of knickers with tight enough elastic in the legs to prevent my embarrassment when the knickers leg dropped to my knees as I ran around. I often had to try numerous pairs of clean knickers on before I found the right fit. Sometimes a friend would throw a pair of knickers in my direction and say, 'Here, these will fit.'

Still naked I would try them on and strut like a model across the landing with the knickers waistline tucked under my armpits, much to the amusement of the other girls and hoping their laughter would not attract the attention of staff.

After finding underwear that did fit me, I would just neatly fold the others up and put them back on the shelf.

Oh my goodness! How disgusting is that?

Thankfully, years later somebody recommended that we should change our underwear twice a week!! They also suggested that we should have our own individually name taped school uniform, home clothes and underwear. I will be forever grateful to whoever came up with that brilliant idea, even though it meant we had to sew all the name tapes onto the clothes ourselves.

15

Sundays

Sundays were always peaceful, tranquil days. The quote of the day was 'Children should be seen and not heard.' We were constantly reminded Sundays were holy days. That meant there was to be no raised voices and no screaming and shouting for the whole day. Apart from the staff of course, they could shout as much as they liked.

The day would begin with an extra hour in bed. Once the member of staff had made sure everyone was awake and the bedroom curtains and windows were wide open, we quickly went through our routine; toilet, get washed and clean our teeth trying not to make a mess. Sunday was our day of rest from housecleaning duties, no sweeping the dorms or washing the bathroom floor.

We dressed into our smart Sunday clothes which we had placed on our bedside chairs the evening before. A strict dress code was in place; girls were not allowed to wear trousers on Sundays. Dresses were worn for the summer months and kilts during winter. The boys wore short trousers, shirt and tie.

At 8:30am some lucky child got to ring the little brass hand bell, kept on the table in the hallway, to indicate it was breakfast time. It was considered quite a triumph to be chosen for that duty. Hearing the bell we would rush to stand behind our chairs until the signal was given for us to sing grace.

Breakfast was usually a bowl of cereal, followed by yummy scrambled egg on toast, with home-made marmalade on toast and a cup of tea. Dining room duty still had to be done. So, the tables had to be cleared, dishes washed and dried then the dining tables were reset ready for lunch.

We then headed for the cloakroom area to get ready for Church. Children under the age of seven did not have to attend the morning service at the Abbey, because the walk was considered to be too far for them. Students from the Hydro College would come and read bible stories and help them to colour in religious pictures. Everyone else went to the Abbey.

We put on our Sunday shoes and donned our navy Burberrys, making sure the belts were fastened correctly with the buckle at the front and not tied at the back as some girls dared to do. It was protocol in those days for everyone to wear a hat for church. All the girls wore coloured berets. Mine was yellow. Oh, and not forgetting to use the toilet, because it could be at least two hours or more before we would get the chance to go again.

Once appropriately dressed, we lined up in pairs beside the back gate ready for inspection. The eldest and tallest children walked at the front, then the younger ones, falling in behind. We stood in silence while the member of staff on duty walked up and down the line tweaking where necessary.

The scrutiny was always followed with her resounding question 'Have you been?' Inevitably, there was always one person we had to wait for.

With everyone at the ready, the member of staff unbolted the small doorway within the huge double back gates and ordered the move forward to the edge of the road. One at a time, we stepped through the doorway. The member of staff then joined the front of the line, and stepped out into the middle of the road, directing the 15 or so navy clad children across. Safely over the road and onto the footpath, we shuffled back into formation and headed towards Hexham with the older children controlling the pace at the front and the member of staff supervising at the rear. The crocodile formation was never broken, as we were frog-marched to church in an orderly manner.

It was imperative we arrived at the Abbey in time for the 11am family service. If we could hear the peal of the Abbey bells, resounding through the town, beckoning the parishioners to join the congregation, we could judge the distance still to go, and increase our pace if necessary to make sure we were not late. On arrival we quietly entered the side entrance door. I loved every aspect of the Abbey.

Stepping inside I was always overwhelmed by the serenity. I loved the architecture and the stained glass windows. The front two rows of pews were always kept empty for us. We collected our hymn books and, as quietly as possible, made our way to our seats.

We had a captive audience. The people already in the congregation would smile and mouth 'Hello' to us and, as instructed, we whispered hello back to them. The older children filed into the back row leaving the front row for the younger ones. The member of staff sat on the end seat in the back row, so she could keep an eye on everyone. Not that we dared to misbehave, especially as we had been warned that God was watching over us.

We heartily sang hymns and joined in with the service where necessary. The older girls knew the hymns and order of service, so only the younger children needed to look at their prayer books. During the sermon, we sat upright and rigid. Slouching or fidgeting was not allowed. At times, we just sat there with a smirk on our faces and discreetly nudged each other as we people-watched.

Once the service was over, we left by the main entrance after shaking hands and smiling politely at the vicar. Then, we quickly shuffled back into an orderly crocodile formation, ready to march back up the hill to the orphanage for lunch. There was no public transport service on Sundays during the 1950's.

When we arrived at the back gate, the smell of the lunch filled the air. We were bursting to use the toilet after the endurance of the past two and a half hours. With Burberrys back on hooks, a quick dash to the toilet and hands washed, we were more than ready for lunch, but, as there was usually half an hour to chill out before lunchtime. That meant doing some more of the 1,000 piece jigsaw always on go, or find a quiet pastimes such as reading, knitting or sewing. Rowdy activities were not permitted on Sundays.

At last, the lunch bell would ring out and we would quietly make our way to the dining room and stand behind our chairs. Sunday lunch times were special for me, because it was the only day of the week I could avoid eating large dollops of turnip. I hated turnip! My hate was exacerbated by my being force fed it, if I had left any on my plate. Eventually I realised if I mixed it with other vegetables, it would make the taste more palatable.

On weekdays, our meals were ready plated up, so there was no asking for a small helping of anything.

We were not allowed to use words such as, 'I don't like.'

Such words triggered a lecture on how ungrateful we were and 'did we not appreciate how lucky we were to have food presented to us, when there were thousands of starving children in the world?' Making the staff rant on like that at everyone made the instigator very unpopular especially if one particular staff member was on duty.

Sunday lunches were delicious. We always had roast meat with two vegetables and one of the cook's special home baked Yorkshire puddings and gravy. The small tables were pushed together and set to enable eight children to sit at each table. Everything looked very splendid with a china gravy boat and tureens with lids, keeping the vegetables and potatoes warm.

After we were given a dinner plate with an exact ration of meat and a Yorkshire pudding on, we then helped ourselves to the trimmings, under a watchful eye to ensure no one was being greedy. The rule was that everyone had to have at least a small portion of everything on their plate.

There was always the fear somebody was watching so we never dared to pass food to another child. Pudding was usually a portion of tinned pears or peaches with jelly and thick lumpy cold custard with skin on. Yuk!! The jug of water on each table was very useful. It meant I could gulp down a glass of water to wash any unsavoury taste in my mouth.

We were forbidden to express emotions of hate on Sundays, but I can safely say now, that I hated being on washing up duty after the meals on Sunday because there were so many extra dishes to wash.

Chores done, it was time for everyone to get ready for our second visit to church at the Methodist Chapel for Sunday-School

Back in the cloakroom, the older children had the responsibility of making sure the younger girls had been to the toilet and were suitably dressed for the weather conditions of the day. If it was dry we wore shoes, if raining, it was wellies. When the younger children were ready, they lined up at the back gate ready for the quick once over. A member of staff guided us safely across the road and we set off up the hill towards the chapel. With the older girls holding hands with a little one as we set off up the hill, with the younger child walking along the inside of the narrow pavement.

The beautiful stone built chapel was just under a mile up the road in the tiny hamlet of Lowgate. Inside the only doorway there was a very small vestibule leading to the main praying area, with a platform area at the front where the organ and lectern were situated. I think there was a big wooden cross leaning against or embedded in the back wall.

The interior was very plain with no fancy altar adorned with gold candlesticks. When I first attended the Chapel it had no electricity and was illuminated by gas lighting. It was fascinating to watch the teacher collect a very long pole with a brass hook on the end and proceed down the centre aisle, reaching up to the chain on the light and, by pulling the chain downwards the gas ignited the bulb and illuminated the shade.

I loved Sunday school, and the lovely middle aged teacher. The atmosphere at the Chapel was enjoyable and relaxing. The hour we were there just flew past. We were told Bible stories about the Disciples. Then we sang some lovely songs printed on a sheet of paper, rather than a hymn book. My favourite was;

Jesus bids a shine, with a pure clear light.
Like a little candle, burning in the night.
In this world is darkness, so let us shine.
You in your small corner and I in mine.

After singing, the older girls would help the younger ones to colour in pictures about the disciple stories. When it was time to go home we always wanted to stay longer. Our lovely teacher Miss Carr lived just a five minute walk further down the road from us, so she quite often walked home with us. Just thinking about those Sunday school days, reminds me of so many happy times.

We usually just got back into the house when the tea time bell would ring out. For tea, we had egg and tomato sandwiches and delicious homemade cakes and a cup of tea. Yet 'another rule' was that you had to eat at least one sandwich before you could have a cake.

Once a month the senior children returned to church a third time, when they attended an Evensong Service held in the small Church of England, situated opposite the Infant School in Lowgate. I can't remember if the service in that tiny church was held on the first or, last Sunday of the month starting at 6pm.

I do recall one particular winters' evening when I was about fourteen though. We'd been advised to wear our wellingtons and wrap up warm against the chilly elements. We set off walking in the pitch black with our heads down, bracing ourselves against the cold wind. It was a time before the luxury of street lighting in rural areas.

Tightly bunched together, we walked towards the lights of the first house on the brow of the hill. Then, we could see the lights of the little church shining in the distance and, could hear the church bell ringing out to let the villagers know the service would soon begin.

As we entered the church, we could feel warm air greeting us, despite there being no heating facilities then. This church was of a similar size to the Methodist chapel but more affluent. The altar was adorned with a silver cross and candlesticks. The service was similar, but less pompous than at the Abbey. We probably made up 50% of the congregation.

As always, we sang the hymns heartily and tried to look interested during the sermon. Extra prayers were said, naming the regular churchgoers if they were poorly, or if any of the parishioners had passed away.

At the end of the service, we were warmly greeted by the vicar and the other worshippers at a little gathering in the vestibule.

We stepped outside the church, straight into a snow storm. The snowflakes were huge and it was snowing so hard we could barely see a hand in front of us. It was an absolute white out.

Although our initial reaction was to squeal and shout about it, we knew if we stuck together we would be fine. The member of staff tried to calm us down and advised us that we should make a human chain by holding each other's hands we set off in the direction of home.

Thank goodness for our navy Burberry, because we could see the dark figures of those in front, against the snowy background. Knowing the route so well meant finding our way back was not a problem. There was plenty of giddiness and shouting on the way home that night. We all totally forgot about the rule.

'No loud voices or shouting on Sundays!'

16

Indoor Activities

Indoor activities were great. There was always something to do which suited most children. There were two very large rooms available to play in, situated at the front of the home with a view overlooking the beautiful rose garden.

Both rooms had parquet flooring, and large tiled fireplaces with mantelpiece surrounding open fires which were lit during winter evenings. Both rooms had huge bay windows draped with floral curtains which made a distinctive swishing sound as the metal rollers were guided along the metal tracking, when a member of staff closed them. Each room was furnished with a large three piece suite generally placed with backs against a wall to allow maximum floor space. A drop leaf dining table and chairs stood close to the windows. The walls were just plastered and painted with a pale-coloured flecked paint.

The noisy room was used for any game requiring interaction such as board games, Ludo, Snakes and Ladders and Draughts, or card games such as Snap and 'Please May I Have.' We also occupied ourselves getting into tangles while playing the Cats' Cradle, using spare wool.

I have forgotten the name of the game we played where we grasped about twenty small sticks together then opened the hand quickly, letting them fall onto a smooth surface. The object of the game was to take it in turns to try and remove one a stick from the pile without disturbing of the others. Obviously the winner was the person with the steadiest hand who had managed to collect the most sticks.

As mentioned previously we generally had a 1,000 piece jigsaw puzzle on the go, in the centre of the table. I still find doing jigsaws therapeutic. There's something satisfying about opening a box containing so many jumbled pieces and eventually creating the beautiful picture within. The younger children had plenty of floor space to play with dolls, cots or prams, and the would-be gymnasts and entertainers had enough space to exhibit their skills.

The quiet room was also used as the staff lounge so it could only be used by children chatting with quiet voices, doing homework or reading.

This room was mainly used by girls sewing name tapes onto clothing or making cotton loops with white tape and sewing them onto our bath towels and flannels. We also embroidered flowers onto the corner of the plain white table cloths.

By the age of ten years old, we were encouraged to switch from knitting squares for blankets and to start knitting our own brown and yellow-striped mittens and scarf in readiness for our senior school uniform. There were hand-me-downs for us to wear if they were not finished by the beginning of the new term. Most of us were skilful knitters and started knitting our own V neck school jumpers.

Then, at the age of eleven, we were knitting socks and mittens, using four small knitting needles. The room was also used if children just wanted a bit of peace, quiet and relaxation. Anyone who dared to raise their voice or be disruptive was banished to the noisy room.

In the huge hallway we sat crossed legged on the floor to watch a black and white television with a very small screen which was encased inside a wooden cabinet with doors.

The BBC was the only television station available in those days. Viewing was strictly controlled, from when we came in from school until teatime. The programmes in the 1950's were Andy Pandy, Muffin the Mule and Noddy, but as the years ticked by, The Whirlybirds, Boots and Saddles and Lassie were introduced.

At some point a more modern television with a larger screen, but still black and white was moved into the room I called the snug, which had previously been used by the staff whilst they were off duty. This room had a comfy settee and chairs for us to sit on, although the younger children still had to sit on the floor. 'The snug' had an upright piano positioned behind the door, so when it wasn't an allocated time for watching television, it was used as a music room. Any of us were allowed to mess about and attempt to play. I think the tune I learned to play was called 'chop sticks.' Priority was always given to the serious players. I was mesmerised listening to one of the girls playing classical music. I thought she was a brilliant musician.

The ballroom was a very large rectangular room, running the full width of the main house with long narrow windows along the three outside walls. The windows were probably draped with the same floral curtains as throughout the house and the walls were just plain, much the same as the other rooms.

I particularly enjoyed the dancing lessons we had in there, when students from the 'Hydro' arrived to teach us. The lessons were such a laugh.

We would giggle so much as they attempted to teach us Ballroom dancing, Scottish dancing and Country dancing. We would be so busy concentrating on our foot movements instead of watching where we were going. It was inevitable we would collide with each other. The lessons generally started in a dignified manner with the waltz or quickstep, but giddiness and excitement soon took over when it was time for country dancing.

The music was provided by one of those old-fashioned wind up gramophones with a chrome bendy arm with a circular contraption at the end securing a very sharp needle. Precision and a steady hand were required to gently place the needle onto the edge of a large 78 record. The place was in an uproar as the record player began winding down causing the music to get slower and slower. We would switch from swinging each other around two by two whilst doing the Gay Gordon to dancing slow motion in time to the decelerating music. A student would race to the gramophone and rapidly start winding the handle to enable the record to play at the correct speed. Then, as the player was being rewound we increased our pace, giggling and laughing uncontrollably as we picked up speed again.

There was a time when the ballroom was strictly for dancing or for use at party times, but that ruling changed after boys became resident and a fold away table tennis table arrived. Until then, I had never heard of table tennis.

At first, I found it difficult trying to bat the ping pong ball over the net to the opponent but I soon learned to enjoy dashing from one side of the table to the other to hit it. Sometimes, the games could be was quite exhausting!

The boys were the skilful players. They seemed to be able to just stand on the same spot and, by stretching to the left or right, accurately return the ball.

Letter writing was another pass-time. Although it was a very rare occurrence for a child to receive post, there was an occasion during 1956 when we were asked if we would like to have a pen friend. This was something I hadn't heard of before and I asked what that meant.

It was explained to me that an organisation arranged for addresses to be exchanged between children who would like to write to each other and ultimately become long distance friends. That sounded a great idea to me, so I said 'Yes.'

I have it fixed in my mind that all post was pre opened and read before being handed over. I clearly recall the letter writing procedure during the era I was living in 'The Cottage'. We were given a piece of scrap paper and pencil to write a draft letter. The emphasis was on telling the recipient some event or news and we had to be sure to answer any questions asked within the pen friend's letter.

After the staff member had approved the contents of the draft we were given a Basildon Bond writing pad and a pen to rewrite the letter neatly. Woe be-tide anyone who messed up on that precious piece of writing paper! After a final inspection of the letter, we addressed the matching envelope and handed it back to staff. I don't recall ever posting the letters.

One day, I was given a letter addressed to me. I excitedly delved into the pre-opened envelope, assuming it was from a new pen friend. Obviously, I don't remember the letter word for word but it began by the person introducing himself, saying he wanted to befriend me and that I could call him Uncle Mac.

Enclosed in this first letter was a piece of white paper with my full name hand written on it and the words Two Shillings and Six Pence printed on the line underneath, I had no idea this piece of paper was of monetary value until a member of staff explained what it was.

I had never seen or heard of a Postal Order before but I did know two shillings and six pence was a lot of money in those days. It was valued at more than a month's pocket money. The staff member could not explain why the money had been sent but did say that the sender was a very generous person. I was overwhelmed with shock and confusion by this letter.

My understanding was that a pen friend would be a child about my age, certainly not someone who could afford to send me money. I couldn't comprehend why this person would want to give me a postal order or why I would need to call him uncle.

In my mind, I already had a lovely, funny Uncle Tom who lived just a couple of streets away from my dad.

I asked a member of staff. 'Why do I need another uncle?' I was dragged to the office to face the Superintendent's wrath. Oh my goodness she was furious! She towered over me as she bellowed at me that I was an ungrateful child and demanded that I should reply immediately to express my gratitude for the generosity and kindness Mr Mc had shown me. It was at this point I realised that this mystery Uncle Mac was a personal friend of hers.

In my records, a comment dated May 1957, states:

It is noted that Mr Mc wishes to take an interest in Marion. He is a bachelor living at the same address as a named female. (The named female was the current Superintendent of the orphanage.)

Another recorded correspondence was between two Barnardo's workers:

Mrs C. thought him to be a very kind and sincere person. But Miss D. rather thought that we might ask Mr Mc to take an interest in the whole family.

However, I could find no record regarding who had authorised that contact should continue. I suspect his friend the Superintendent had the last word.

I find it strange that the first entry, on my retrieved 'Correspondence and Visits' record shows a letter received from the person I called Uncle Mac on 8th May 1958, a year after his first letter. However, I realise that it is possible 'Contact Sheets' were only introduced at that time.

I don't remember the actual date he made the journey from London to meet me but the impact of that first meeting has never left me. It was Saturday morning and I had been excused from doing house duties and was ordered to wear smart clothes. There was a buzz in the house because visitors usually arrived by the bus load. It was a very rare occurrence for any individual child to have a visitor.

Mid-morning, I was summoned to the superintendent's office. With a rare smile on her face, she introduced me to a very tall, very old-looking man with grey, greasy hair. His right arm outstretched towards me, beckoning me to step forward and shake his hand.

Approaching him, I noticed his index and middle fingers were a strange orange colour and there was an overwhelming repulsive stench filling my nostrils. Trying to disguise my disgust, I stretched out my hand to reach his and winced at the roughness of the palm of his hand. As instructed earlier, I said, 'Pleased to meet you sir,' and 'Thank you for your kindness.'

We were then ushered to the play-room where I was expected to have a conversation with him. I have no idea what was said that day. The door had been left open so other children were running into the room. Visibly shocked to see I had a visitor, apologising for interrupting and going straight out again. I was longing for one of them to stay and rescue me from the uncomfortable situation I found myself in. I don't recall how long the visit lasted, or whether he had his meals with us, I was just so relieved when the visit was over. There was nobody for me to confide in, and I didn't dare say I felt very uncomfortable in his presence.

Uncle Mac's letter writing and monthly weekend visits continued until February 1960. He then wrote to a Miss D. at Barnardo's Head Quarters in London asking for an interview with her to explain his request for my visit to London. In my notes I discovered that correspondence continued between Miss D. and a Mr S:

Mr Mc called in to see you this afternoon, and in your absence I spoke to him. Apparently, Mr Mc, who is a single man, aged about 65 was put in touch with Marion through the Sunday Pictorial in Mrs H's time, and he has visited the child several times and has written frequently.

Mr Mc's request is that Marion can go to friends of his, named Mrs P for as many holidays as she is able, so that he and Mrs P can take her on holidays etc. I explained to him the difficulties of a single man making these proposals and he said that Marion must be entirely in the care of Mrs P. Marion is only 13 years old and explained to him that a very thorough investigation would have to be made.

A letter from Barnardo's Northern office Case Department dated 29th March 1960:

Requesting a welfare-officer visit Mrs P in London, to discuss the idea with them that Marion should spend the holidays with them whenever she was able. As she is only thirteen years of age, it would of course also be necessary for her to be escorted on this (A post note on the records states, the second page to this letter is not on file.)

Other comments state: *Mr Mc seems extremely generous, as he has given Marion quite a number of nice presents and has also made one or two nice gifts to the Hexham Branch Home.*

I did have that holiday in London and stayed with Mrs P and her family.

Naturally, it was an exciting time for me. Being collected from the orphanage, and taken on a steam train to London to see where the Queen lived and watching the spectacular formation of the changing of the guards at Buckingham

Palace. We also visited museums and most of London's main attractions, all expenses paid.

So how could I dare tell anyone I had a great adventure but felt uncomfortable in his presence, especially as the adults responsible for me had sanctioned the trip?

The following year, Uncle Mac asked for permission for me to join him on holiday to Folkestone in Kent. Not wanting to be alone with him, I asked if one of my roommates could come with me on holiday. To my surprise, everyone concerned agreed with my request. While enjoying our first beach holiday, we were also taken by ferry on a day trip to Calais, which was a very exciting experience for two young orphans.

Although Uncle Mac was always kind, my first impressions of him have never left me. I still remember my embarrassment when I saw the way people looked at us when we were out and about together and I squirmed when he attempted to hold my hand or put his hand on my shoulder. Human contact with adults was alien to me. I hadn't been raised in an environment with tactile people. Consequently, I couldn't bare him touching me.

This whole scenario made me feel trapped within a difficult predicament.

17

Outdoor Activities

We spent many hours playing in the beautiful rambling grounds of the home.

I don't recall the staff telling us that we couldn't play out because of weather conditions. Rain, hail, snow or sunshine, it didn't matter to most of us. We just wanted the freedom of being outside.

Staying indoors on sunny days was forbidden, or should I say strongly discouraged. The children who didn't want to play out could occupy themselves in the large outdoor cloakroom area of the main house or the garage attached to 'The Cottage' situated behind the main building.

They were great areas to play if the elements were too cold or wet to be outside. For me, every available opportunity to be outdoors was taken. Once in from school, we changed out of our school uniform into outdoor clothes and played out until the huge church-like bell above the back door rang out.

There was no distinction between boys and girls games, we just played together. Danger never seemed to be an issue or concern to us. We took turns to climb the trees in the grounds, to see who dared reach the greatest height. The children who preferred not to climb often became our cheer leaders, encouraging the climbers by shouting from below.

Scrambling to the top of a tree was easy because you could see and reach up to the branch above, but coming back down was the tricky bit. If we got stuck or couldn't see or feel the next branch down, the support group below would shout instructions to direct us to a safe footing.

I don't remember any serious accidents or injuries whilst climbing; just a few scratches. There was only one rule. Never climb trees if the branches were wet and slippery. I was never sure if that was one of our own rules, or one of theirs.

Of course the boys thought they were the best climbers, but occasionally they met their match. Me! I loved hanging upside down by the knees from the most outreaching and highest branch, dangling into space, looking at the amazing upside-down scenery beyond the boundary wall. Swaying in the treetops was so exhilarating, gave me a sense of freedom and made me feel invincible.

We did not have swings like those in parks of today. We had rope swings, either just a knotted rope tied to a branch of a tree or a rope with a wooden plank tied to the end for us to straddle our legs, then sit and swing.

While the adventurous daredevils were climbing trees and swinging from ropes, the children who were not keen on running around often just sat on the boundary wall, waving at the drivers of the occasional passing car or lorry.

Others played more sedate games, like making dens in the shrubbery or playing marbles, hide and seek, kick the can, statues, leap frog, tig, ball games or skipping. We also enjoyed playing statues. The object of the game was to be the first person to creep up and touch the child standing facing the wall. Some of the children found it very difficult to stand motionless and stop laughing when the person with their back to us, suddenly turned round.

Lengths of washing line were used as our skipping ropes. We took it in turns to be at the end of the rope doing the turning. The two children turning the rope stood about six feet apart turning the rope and the 'enders,' as we called them, got to choose the skipping songs. A favourite at the time was:

'Charlie Chaplin went to France, to teach the ladies how to dance.
First they did the rumba. Then they did the kicks.
Then they did the Highland fling. Then they did the splits'.

The children skipping in the middle of the rope, about eight boys and girls would be doing the actions to the dances whilst singing.

Some of the skipping games were more adventurous, especially when we played double rope skipping. This required two people standing apart with a rope in each hand. 'The enders' needed to have fairly strong arms and shoulders for the constant swinging of the ropes in momentum, by swinging the rope in the right hand towards the left, then, immediately swinging the left hand rope to the right. Once the ropes were being turned in unison, about four skippers would carefully watch for the split-second gap, then, run between the ropes into the centre. Everyone would start singing another favourite song:

'On a mountain, stands a lady, who she is I do not know.
All she wants is gold and silver. All she wants is a nice young man.

So, call in my, ... dear, while I go home for tea.'

The person skipping would then call a boy's name out. If the boys weren't playing, a girl's name would be called out instead. Whoever's name was called out, then, had to run into the centre of the ropes. It really was quite tricky running in and out of two fast-moving ropes.

After the younger children had returned to their respective houses, the older children played a very dangerous game. We would stand in a circle with our feet together. The starter of the game would hold the blade of an open penknife and throw it to stick in the ground a few inches in front or behind the person beside them. That person then had to take a step to place their foot near the penknife. Then, it was their turn to throw the knife in front or behind the person beside them. Of course it was inevitable there would be accidents, but nobody made a fuss about it.

When the knife struck my leg, we just rushed to the cloakroom to try and stop the blood flow. The crinkly Izal toilet paper was useless at absorbing the blood but with the combination of nipping the wound together and the freezing cold water, the bleeding soon stopped. Then, I placed clean pieces of toilet paper over the wound and pulled my knee socks over it. Eventually, I had to have the wound dressed properly but, told a fib to staff about how it had happened. Looking at the scar today, I realise it probably needed stitches.

There was always something different to do in the grounds. We had a lawn tennis court which was kept neatly manicured during the tennis season by the resident gardener. He was responsible for assembling the net and winding the tension handles at each side until the net was taut enough for us to play.

We played for hours, taking turns to use the wooden-framed tennis racquets and bright white tennis balls. When we had finished playing, we gathered the balls and made sure they were all accounted for, then released the tension of the net, by unwinding the handles at each end of the wooden supports, then, placed the tennis racquets in their square wooden frames. We could also play ball games on the lawn but, football was prohibited.

At the edge of the lawn, there was a large pond for us to play in on hot summer evenings. The girls wore brightly-coloured, wrinkled nylon stretch bathing costumes. Once issued with a costume, it lasted us for years, because it just stretched and grew with us. The boys wore amusing, skimpy, Speedo type trunks.

The concrete pool wasn't very deep, probably only knee height but I had great fun diving under the water and trying to swim. I don't think we had towels for drying by the pool. We probably just ran around until we were dry. If we sat quietly, close to the pool, we would see beautiful colourful dragon flies, swooping and skimming the water.

When I was about seven, a local farmer gave us an orphaned lamb to look after. We called her Katy and took turns to feed her milk from a bottle with a large teat. Then, as she got older, she happily grazed in her small paddock just outside the dining room windows. At that time, we thought she knew her name because, when we called for her, she would bleat and run towards us.

Now of course, I understand that she was only rushing to be fed! Sadly, one day on our return from school, Katy was missing. We searched the grounds for her thinking she had been moved to another grazing area but, alas, we were told Katy had gone home. She was a lovely fat, cuddly beast. I really missed her.

At some time around 1960, a new Superintendent arrived to take over the running of Mount Royal, I thought he must have been a farmer because he cordoned off an area of the grounds to keep pigs.

There were two or three pig sties, and we enjoyed taking turns to feed them with vegetable peelings and leftover food. I loved watching the piglets grow.

It may be a coincidence, but, about the same time of the new Superintendent arrival, the local land owner and horse trainer, very kindly fenced off a section of his field, adjacent to the grounds of Mount Royal and allowed us to use it as an extended playing field. His generosity caused great excitement, especially for the boys who tried on many occasions to claim this extended playing area as their football pitch.

I am sure we must have been supervised from a distance, but I never saw a member of staff watching over us. I don't remember being told not to play any particular game or to quieten down. We would play out until the large bell above the back door rang out for meal time. We then dashed to the cloakroom to clean up before our entering the house.

I really cherish the memories of those happy, carefree days.

18

Long Walks

I have so many happy memories of the times we were taken on long walks. I assume this was to get us out of the house or prevent us from being bored during the school holidays. There is a strong possibility that I was always the first to jump up with excitement when a member of staff announced that we would be going for a walk after lunch.

The distance of these treks varied from between three and eight miles. The eight mile circular route took us a few miles up the road towards Allendale, then, after taking a left turn, onto a lane which passed the Hexham Race Course, down into Hexham and back up the hill to the home again. Of course we avoided that particular walk whenever there was a race meeting.

As always while being supervised, we walked in normal crocodile style until we ran out of footpath at the Lowgate junction, then crossed over to the right hand side of the main road so we were facing any oncoming traffic. We continued our journey on the grass verge, passing the outer edge of the Infant school playing field and the little church we attended for evensong which stood on the opposite side of the road. Though still keeping close together, we were now allowed to break formation.

There was plenty of activity going on in the surrounding countryside to distract us on route. I can still visualise the spectacular sight of two magnificent cart horses pulling a hand held plough guided by a farmer. It was remarkable to see how straight the plough troughs were. I wondered where all the seagulls swooping towards the ground came from and, questioned why they were called seagulls when we lived miles away from the sea?

Reaching the turn off for the country lane which accessed the race course, we were supervised across a main road then, given permission to run freely.

This expanse of lane was good for finding different types of wild flowers. When we reached an area close to the actual race course, there was a gap in the hedgerow where we could clearly see the orphanage in the distance. Some of us would stand as high as we could on the fence and frantically shout and wave to see if any of the younger children left behind could see us looking down on them. There were occasions when we could see children sitting on the boundary wall, waving in our direction but I'm not sure they could really see us at that distance. We were ordered to get down from the fence because it was time to set off for the trek back to the home.

Passing the entrance to the race course was of no interest to me, I knew horses ran around a field but, that was the extent of my knowledge then.

I remember chasing rainbows in that lane. We could see the end of a beautiful rainbow in the distance, so we ran as fast as we could, thinking we would find the pot of gold at the end of it. But, the faster we ran towards it, the further it moved away from us. We never did find the pot of gold.

The lane continued until it joined a main road on the outskirts of Hexham. We shuffled back into formation, then, walked downhill all the way towards the town, until we reached the junction with the Allendale road. Sometimes, our tired legs struggled to cope with the final uphill stage back to the home.

The six miles to Elrington Moor was a lovely walk. It started as a mixed age group walk. As usual we set off in formation but once across the main road at Lowgate, we were free to break ranks and run freely along the road past the infant school, towards the Elrington Moor junction. This unclassified road had no centre-line white markings and, as there were very few cars then, we ran freely whilst listening and watching for the occasional farm vehicles.

I don't remember if we took a packed lunch or water with us for our walks, although, it is possible the member of staff could have carried sandwiches. I certainly have no recollection of carrying food or, stopping for a picnic.

However, I do remember that while out on our walks we foraged for wild seasonal fruit growing in the hedgerow. Just a short distance from the school, there was a farmers trail to the left, and for obvious reasons, we called it Crab Apple Lane. That area was a great place to find blackberries, gooseberries and raspberries.

On one occasion, when I was happily stuffing myself with raspberries, one of the older children laughed and asked, 'How many maggots have you eaten?' Horrified and immediately spitting my mouthful out onto the ground, I replied, 'What?' Still laughing, she warned me to be careful and check inside the raspberry before eating it, because, sometimes they had maggots hiding inside them. Sure enough, peering at the next raspberry I was about to eat, I saw a wriggly maggot inside. No, I didn't throw it away. I merely removed the maggot, and ate the raspberry.

We soon learned the dire consequences of eating too many crab apples and that complaining to staff when we got belly ache was pointless, because, we were just be told 'It's your own fault.' We certainly did not get any sympathy. We gathered apples and left them at the side of the road, in readiness to collect on our way home, so for our cook to make delicious crab-apple jelly.

A large hut on the right-hand side of the road was used by the lovely ladies of Lowgate Women's Institute, who very kindly donated clothes, gifts and toys to the children at Mount Royal. I hope the WI ladies attending while I was a resident in the 1950's were aware that their generosity was appreciated.

Alongside their hut, we could see delicious plums hanging from the branches. Oh my! They were so very tempting, but we were ordered not to pick plums from the tree because the ladies needed them to make jam to sell at their Autumn Fayre. So, as we were obedient children, especially if we were being watched, we rummaged for windfalls and ate them instead!

When we reached the junction for Elrington Moor, the children were divided into two groups. The final stretch of the walk was reserved for the children attending senior school only. The juniors about turned and headed back to the home, usually escorted by one of the very senior girls, who had just left school and was about to venture into the outside world.

My records reveal on 1st January 1958, my elder sister June, was a member of staff at Mount Royal, when she was sixteen years old. So, it is possible that she may have done one of those escort duties. Sadly, June died before I got the opportunity to ask her what responsibilities her staff position had entailed.

The seniors eagerly picked up their pace and resumed their journey to the moor with the member of staff. On this section of road, we saw cows walking in a line through their field as they headed towards the farm to be milked and we looked with interest as we passed each field, noticing how much the crops had grown, since the last time we had seen them. There were fields with turnips, potatoes, cabbages, sprouts and broad beans.

While some of the children ran on ahead, a few of us would sit on the stone wall and watch a farmer as he cut the grass using a very long handled scythe. It was fascinating to watch him twisting his upper body sideways before swinging the scythe to the front of him, slicing through the long grass as he slowly walked through the field. His children or helpers would follow behind him, raking the cut grass into piles. All the farmers in the area knew where we were from and always waved when they saw us.

It was great fun when we finally reached the moor. We played hide and seek in the heather, but, a few children were afraid of the grass snakes lurking there. I thought the snakes were probably more frightened of us rowdy kids invading their territory, they were well camouflaged which made them difficult to find when we hunted for them. The rabbits ran for their lives as we approached them. We saw sparrow-hawks, lapwings and the curlews with beautiful long beaks flying around the moor.

None of us had any sense of time, so, a groan of disappointment filled the air when the order to head back was given. We linked arms and skipped to the beat while we sang one of our favourite song, 'I love to go a wandering,' and, continued singing and dancing our way back along the road in the direction of where we had left the pile of apples. Then, we scooped them up into the upturned bottom of our blouse or tee shirts and cradled them at our waistline until we arrived back home and delivered them to our cheerful cook at the kitchen door.

The shortest of our regular walks, covering about three miles, was done by all age groups of children, including the infants. Starting at Lowgate, we ventured down the country back lane running down the side of the Methodist church. Long before the caravan park was established or the extra houses were built, that lane was a beautiful and cultivated mile-long thoroughfare for farming vehicles, passing between the A69 Carlisle road and the Lowgate/Allendale B6305 road junction. We would walk from the orphanage in our two by two crocodile fashion, but, once in the lane, permission was given to run freely.

I was saddened on a recent visit to see that the lane was now overgrown and neglected. I have so many happy memories of great adventures in that lane. We would dart from side to side searching for wild flowers.

There was great excitement if we met the farmer herding his cattle or sheep from one field to another. We tried to muffle our screams as we pressed ourselves against the stone walls flanking the lane as the animals passed by. The sheep were always the noisiest, loudly bleating as they moved by, but the cattle were the smelliest, making fresh cow pats as they walked past us.

I remember a time when we saw lots of dead rabbits just lying in the lane staring into space with their milky-coloured glazed eyes wide open. Naturally, we were told not to touch them because they had a disease called Myxomatosis. But, we were drawn to them and couldn't resist poking them with a stick to check they were really dead.

Half way down the lane there was a wooded area, I don't know its official name, but we knew it as 'Blue Bell' woods for obvious reasons. That was a great area to play hide and seek and climb trees.

Recently my sister reminded me of the occasion our play came to an abrupt end when we spotted a man hiding in the woods. We reported our sighting to the member of staff who promptly gathered us all together and said we must return to the home immediately. We were very disgruntled and walked slowly as we headed back up the lane, until we spotted two policemen, wearing what we used to call 'Noddy' hats, heading towards us.

They asked if we had seen anyone in the lane. We eagerly informed them about the man hiding in the woods and described what he was wearing. They thanked us and walked on. Our pace then increased as we hurried back to the orphanage to share our exciting news.

Later that day, there was even more excitement when we saw a dark blue Bedford van heading up the driveway. As it got close we realised it was a Police van. A member of staff met the officer at the front door and ushered him into the office. He emerged after a short while and the staff member escorted him back to his van. They walked to the back of the van, he then opened the door, and handed her a big cardboard box before getting back in his the van and driving off.

As always, not wanting to miss a trick, we were peering from behind the curtains of the playing room, trying to guess what was going on. Eventually, we were informed the man we'd spotted in the woods had now been captured and arrested.

The cardboard box contained ice-cream. It was gift to us all from the officers, to thank us for helping them to find the escaped prisoner.

That was my most adventurous walk!

19

The Shoe Cupboard

The girls generally wore Clarks brown T-bar sandals fastened with a buckle during the summer school term and switched to brown lace-up shoes for the winter. Our shoes were expected to last us for at least a full school term. If our shoes had become shabby or too small, we sometimes encountered difficulty trying to convince a member of staff we needed a replacement pair.

The general rule was that children up to the age of eleven were supervised and helped by a member of staff when finding a suitable change, but that didn't always happen. Occasionally, we were supervised by a senior girl. Older children could be accompanied by a friend.

The shoe cupboard was moved to various locations during my time in residence. The least favourable location was when the shoes were kept in the cold, smelly, creepy cellar. Immediately the door was unlocked and opened, an overpowering smell of dampness filled the air. It was freezing cold and so scary down there. It was paramount to quickly find a pair of shoes that fit and get out of there as soon as possible.

I preferred the huge walk-in cupboard, situated at the bottom of the stairs used by the staff to reach their living quarters, We could try shoes on in a more relaxing atmosphere there. The layout of the room was similar to that of the cellar, with a shelf running the full length of the room which housed rows of highly polished second-hand brown lace up school shoes or tan sandals, as well as black lace-up shoes for the boys. Under the shelf standing upright like soldiers, stood rows of black knee length wellingtons and a big box of black plimsolls, or pumps as we called them. They were worn for PE lessons and as our indoor shoes.

This shoe cupboard also had fancy party shoes, black or red patent leather shoes the likes of which I had never seen before. Whilst looking for replacement school shoes, I couldn't resist the temptation of trying to squeeze my feet into the beautiful shiny party shoes and hoping they would still be on the shelf in December, which was the only month of the year such shoes were worn.

When that day finally arrived if we were lucky enough to find a pair of party shoes, they could only to be worn with our party dresses during the Christmas party season. Then, sadly, they were wiped clean and returned to the shelf for some other lucky person to wear the following Christmas.

It appears I may have paid the price for not wearing correctly fitted shoes. My memory of why and how it became apparent I needed to have corrective surgery is a little sketchy. I do remember a local doctor visited the orphanage now and then to check the general health of the residents.

I can visualise him sitting in the bay window of the quiet playing room as he watched me walk around bare footed. Then, examining my feet, he gently tried to manoeuvre my big toes back into their sockets, but they just settled back to what had become their normal position.

After several check-ups and an appointment with an Orthopaedic Surgeon, it was decided I needed to have corrective surgery on both feet for bunions. So, on 4th March 1961, at just thirteen years old, I was admitted to Hexham War Memorial Hospital.

At that time the wards were still little prefabricated huts. The hospital ward was an open-plan area with at least eight beds. I have no recollection of spending the night in hospital before my surgery. I'm convinced the new Superintendent of the orphanage (who owned a car) took me to the hospital that morning, a short while before my scheduled surgery.

However I do have a vivid memory of waking up in the ward crying and feeling so much pain, I thought my feet had been cut off. Looking downwards, I could only see the bed sheet covering a box shaped gadget. I must have been causing a fuss because a nurse wearing a dark blue dress and a crisp white apron and starched hat came to see me.

She smiled, lifted the sheet to reassure me that my feet were still there, explaining that 'the cage.' as she called it was over my feet to protect them from the heavy blankets.

Checking my feet were still there, I could see they were both wrapped in firm plaster casts from toes to ankle. My feet felt as though they were a ton weight.

Glancing around the ward I could see weird contraptions attached to some of the beds. One of the patients seemed to have a rope tied around his ankle, which in turn appeared to be connected to a pulley apparatus with weights attached. Another patient had her arm trussed upwards by a similar device. That was a very scary vision for a young girl.

The first week in hospital was so monotonous because I was confined to my bed the whole time. I particularly hated using those freezing cold metal bed pans, which instantly stopped the flow of any normal bodily function. The time just dragged by.

I have no recollection of having visitors. None of my friends could visit, because children were not allowed to visit hospital patients in those days. All my elder siblings had already left the orphanage so I assumed they were unable to visit me, and have no memory of any visits. However, when checking my Visitors Record, retrieved within my Barnardo's notes, I discovered both my sisters had visited me on several occasions after my surgery. In fact, during my long convalescing time, all my siblings who had lived in the orphanage managed to visit me.

Ten or twelve days after surgery, the casts were cut off and the stitches were carefully taken out. Once the clean dressings were in place, the warm soft plaster bandage was wrapped around my big toes to hold them in the correct position. Then a green rubber heels device was secured under the arches of my feet by the plaster cast bandage, before they continued wrapping the bandage around my legs, right up to my knees. When the technicians were finished plastering, I was lifted into a wheelchair and taken back to the ward. Now those plaster casts really did seem to be like a ton weight!

During my last few days in hospital, I learned how to balance on the green heel structures and walk, or should I say 'waddle,' my way from one bed to another. My instructions were to stand bolt upright, find my balance and take a step forward. Learning to walk again was an exhausting task. I don't recall being offered any wooden crutches to support me under the arms. I am surmising that once I could balance and walk a short distance I was discharged, and given an appointment for having my plasters removed.

Although I wasn't due to move into the bungalow until the start of the September 1961 school term, a place was found for me in March. Of course I knew the girls already living in the bungalow doing their final two years at the orphanage preparing for the outside world.

Obviously, the early move meant it was more convenient for me to avoid climbing stairs. I was delighted to be moving in, because my favourite member of staff was in charge of the bungalow. It was only ten days until my fourteenth birthday, and I considered that placement to be my best-ever birthday present. Whenever I needed to walk around, there was always a helping hand nearby, as all 'inmates' were eager to help out.

I definitely missed going to school for the next six weeks and I am sure there was no school work being sent for me. The staff had time off duty while the children were at school so I went to the main house and sat around knitting most of the day.

Until having that time off school, I had no idea how many busloads of visitors came during school hours, although I did understand they just wanted to see where their gifts and donations were going. I wish I had been given sixpence for every time a visitor asked. 'Have you been run over?'

Having to explain what had happened to me became quite tedious.

While I was still wearing the plaster casts, a group of us from the orphanage were confirmed at Hexham Abbey, and, because I was unable to walk to the Alter and kneel, the Bishop had to come to the front row where I was sitting. He confirmed and blessed me there. Then, he continued the service.

I was so excited when it was finally time for those heavy plaster casts to be cut off because that meant no more 'up and under' washing in the bathroom! At last, I could look forward to having a bath. So, the plasters came off and I had my lovely bath.

Surprisingly, within a couple of months, my big toes slipped back to their pre-operative position and they have stayed like that to this day.

No, I don't think what a waste of time, because since then I have had no problem running several marathons and half marathons, and I still play Squash and Badminton.

I now know that when such surgery is carried out today, the big toe is generally held into position, with a small metal plate or screws. I am also aware that having bunions can be caused a hereditary abnormality, which can be exacerbated by wearing ill fitted shoes.

20

Home Visits

Reading my records revealed that during early 1955, I discovered there was correspondence from my father to Barnardo's requesting that I join my elder brothers and sisters for their annual summer holiday visit to our family home.

I was eight years old when the request was made, and was blissfully unaware that I had not been to the family home since the death of my mother in 1948. And, I had absolutely no idea my brothers and sisters had been visiting dad during the summer holidays since 1952.

I'm not sure when my brothers Albert and Douglas first went home for visits, because their orphanages were located just a few miles from dad's house in Backworth. They were living close enough to have visited dad at any time.

Dad's request for me to stay with him caused a debate about whether I was old enough to face up to the realisation there would be no mother at home to look after me while he was at work. There were also concerns about whether the family house was adequate for us all to live in for two weeks.

An inspection of dad's house raised worries about the house being a little unkempt and that it would be overcrowded, but, eventually, permission was granted on the proviso that my eldest sister Audrey, whom I had yet to meet, was at the family home to look after and supervise us.

I was very surprised to read in my records that I had been spending my summer breaks up to then with a new foster family and, that they had wanted to foster me on a permanent basis but their request had been refused.

I had no idea how we got to dad's house until one of my sisters told me that our eldest brother Bob was given time off work from the local farm so he could collect us from Hexham and take us there. Apparently, the car had long bench seats in the front and the back, with fold away seats behind the driver and front passenger, to enable all of us to fit in comfortably.

I can't imagine it being Bob's car, because he was only a 24 year old farm assistant and men had to be very rich to own a car in those days. My dad certainly didn't own a car.

It saddens me that no matter how hard I try, I have no recollection of that first long journey home or meeting my dad for the first time, although I do recall being a little apprehensive about who this person called 'dad' was and what he was like.

I don't recall my home visits on a day to day basis but I do have certain memories which are imprinted in my mind, especially the one when we all walked to the bus stop at the edge of the housing estate to meet him getting off the pit bus. He was still wearing his dirty work clothes with his metal knee caps strapped to his knees.

That vision really shocked me because I had never seen anyone looking so dirty before. He was covered from head to toe in soot, the whites of his eyes shone and when he smiled his teeth looked so white. Sadly, I have no recollection of him ever visiting me at either Orphanage. For me, this was the first time I had met him.

We always entered our house by the back door. I still remember the peculiar odour that greeted us as we stepped into the kitchen. Standing at the doorway and looking to the left, I could see one of those tall, slim, 1950's kitchen units with glass cupboard doors at the top and a centre panel that pulled downwards to make a work shelf, then plain double doors under the shelf to store the crockery. I think there was a grey fleck coloured gas cooker with four top burners and a high level grill standing next to the unit. I clearly remember there was always a well-used chip pan standing on one of the burners.

Looking to the right, I remember an enamel sink under the window and a shelving unit where the pans were hidden behind a blue floral curtain. I asked why the sink was piled up with dirty dishes, because we had been taught that dishes were to be washed immediately after use.

Audrey quickly replied it was because the dishes were only washed once a day to save the hot water. Beside the sink, there was one of those old fashioned washing machines with a mangle, and a large metal object hanging on the wall just to one side.

Continuing with my questioning, I asked what this thing was. Audrey informed me that, if dad didn't have time to clean up before he came home from the pit, he used the tin bath to save the new white bath upstairs, from getting a black sooty rim around it. I had never seen a bath like that before.

Along the wall behind the back door there were cupboard doors standing ajar. Investigating, I could see a coal house and a walk-in pantry with coat hooks inside the door. It didn't take long to discover the source of that strange pong. It was coming from the gas meter hidden in the cavity under the stairs, alongside the electric meter.

We would take turns to crawl into the tiny space to place a large old brown penny into the gas meter slot and turn the small handle until we heard the penny drop into the metal box below. The electric meter needed half a crown (or two and sixpence in old money) to make the lights come on again. That was the first time I became aware that gas and electricity had to be paid for.

Moving from the kitchen to the living room, I first caught sight of one of those long sticky fly papers hanging from a bare light bulb attached to the ceiling fitting. It must have been hanging there for a while. The paper was almost black because it had so many flies stuck to it!

There was a huge black range dominating the centre of the fireplace wall. It had an open coal fire to the right and an oven section to the left, with a brass bar running the full length of the mantelpiece, used for airing things, usually had my dad's pit socks hanging from it.

A large black kettle sat on a brass gadget that swung the kettle over the flames when we needed hot water for a cup of tea. A black companion set and a large coal scuttle stood at one end of the tiled hearth.

In the centre of the room stood a large-dark wood dining table surrounded by half a dozen chairs with leather covered seats. One of my sisters informed me there was a black prickly chaise-longue hidden behind the dining table but I have no memory of that. In the corner, close to the window, was a small table with a wooden wireless standing on it.

I don't remember hearing music being played but I do recall hearing a very distinctive voice saying 'This is the BBC News.' There might have been a television, but I have no memory of watching it. Continuing through the living room, there was a door leading to the bottom of the stairs and to the front door, which was always locked and bolted. Then, there was a downstairs room where dad slept but I never went in there.

Upstairs, there were three bedrooms. My brothers slept in the room used by our elder brothers who had stayed at home to live with dad after our mother died. I had thought they were both away doing their compulsory National Service, but my sister has since told me that Thomas did not do National Service so I have no idea where he was. However, I do know that I didn't meet either of them, during my first home visit.

Another room with a double bed in it seemed so cramped, I could hardly open the door to look in. That room was being used by my eldest sister Audrey who was just fourteen years old when mam died. She was kept off school and, with very little help, took over the responsibility of looking after eight younger siblings for ten weeks, until the five youngest children were placed into the care of Barnardo's. Now 21 years old, married with children of her own, she had kindly returned to the family home to look after us for two weeks of the summer holidays so we could visit dad.

I shared a room with my sisters. We slept top to tail in a double bed, two at the top and, of course, me being the youngest I had to sleep at the bottom. I remember that experience so well because, no matter which way I turned during the night, I constantly had smelly feet in my face.

The bathroom had a washbasin, bath and toilet with a high level cistern with a long chain to pull for flushing. A big copper hot water tank stood behind the base of the bath. There were occasions we ran out of toilet paper and so we used newspaper cut into squares, used a screwdriver to bore a hole into one corner of the layers, thread string through then hang the paper onto the toilet roll hook. Although it was softer than the usual Izal toilet paper, I hated wiping myself with the newspaper because the black print used to come off.

It was a weird and confusing meeting Bob and Audrey for the first time and being told they were my elder siblings. Obviously they had met me when I was born and knew me for the first eighteen months of my life but I was eight years old by then and had no memory of them. I never knew they existed until that first visit.

I was pleased they were my older siblings though, because I did understand that, without them, my visit would not have been possible.

Audrey was quite a serious person. On reflection, that was probably due to her childhood coming to an abrupt end when she took on adult responsibilities at just fourteen. Robert, or Bob as we knew him, was a lively character. I never knew if he was being serious or joking. I laughed so much when he told me my name was supposed to be April. I already have sisters called May, born in May, and June, born in June. Bob said I was due to be born in April so my mother had intended to call me April, but, when I arrived unexpectedly on 30th March, my name was changed to Marion. Thank goodness my name isn't March. It shocked me to learn that I was my mother's 10th single child born within sixteen years. (Bless her).

During my subsequent three home visits, I met my elder brothers Matthew and Thomas but I didn't get to know them very well. I also had an opportunity to meet my sister Olive, who was named after my mother. Olive was always smart and wore very trendy clothes. I was fascinated by her fashionable spectacles. She could attach different coloured plastic pieces into the framework just above her eyes. So for example, if she wore a turquoise coloured dress or jumper, she put in a turquoise piece. She could change the colour to match any outfit she wore. What a brilliant idea!

Dad lived on a council estate called Castle Square. It was a quadrant of houses with a lovely playing field in the middle. Our house was just a few doors away from the green. Everyone on the estate knew who we were, possibly because we wore smart clothes which made us stand out from the other children. I was often asked if I was one of Jakie Thompson's kids. That was dad's nick name. His real name was Jacob.

My siblings were responsible for my every move. Not that I ventured far on that first visit. I spent most of my time playing on the green. This was a very exciting time for me. I had played with lots of children before but I had never played outside the confinement of the orphanage boundary wall or the school playground. It felt like I was living in a whole new world. We played for hours with the other kids on the estate. I learned new versions of games to those we had played at the Orphanage.

Of course we had played tig many times, but never Catchy Kissy!! I didn't like that game very much because some of the boys doing the catching and kissing had a peculiar smell about them and were a bit slobbery. So, I used to make up an excuse to play something else or to go back home.

It was a strange experience not to live by rules, or, be controlled by a bell ringing. I didn't seem to care what time it was or if I had missed a meal time. Audrey would just give us something to eat whenever we turned up at the door hungry.

Meal times were different to those we were used to. Breakfast was cereal and then toast done by securing a slice of bread onto a toasting fork and holding it close to the flames from the hot coals on the fire. In fact at eight years old I had never seen how toast was made because I was used to toast just being presented to me already made. At lunchtime we had jam and bread or sugar sandwiches. As a child I loved those sugar sandwiches.

Now that was a treat we never had at the orphanage. Our main meal in the evening was generally fried egg or sausage with beans, chips and bread and butter. Occasionally, we had shepherds' pie or beef stew.

I was amazed and scared the first time I watched Audrey peel a potato and cut it into chips. She held the potato firmly in the palm of her hand while she sliced it four times from top to bottom with a sharp knife, then, by twisting her wrist slightly cut four times through those slices. I was terrified she would cut through her hand but she never did.

The smell of the boiling fat was pretty disgusting and I was afraid of the sizzling and splashing of the hot fat as the cold potatoes were lowered into the chip pan. I had never seen chips being made before. The cook used to make them for us and hand them through the hatch already on a plate. This was also the first time I'd been introduced to a chip butty.

Yes, I'd had chips on many occasions but at the orphanage we were never allowed to squash them into a piece of bread or bread bun to make a chip butty. I'd never had pop either.

While trying to drink pop for the first time, I could feel the fizz going up my nose as I lifted the beaker to my mouth. Taking a mouthful, I started coughing and spluttering. I was sure I was about to choke to death but my brothers and sisters were doubled up laughing as they just slapped me on the back.

It was a great estate to be on. There was always something going on for us to see or do. Many tradesmen came onto the estate by horse and cart. They rang a little bell shouting 'Fruit and Veg,' or 'any kind of pop,' so the householders knew what they were selling. When the children heard the tradesman's call, they ran into the street with a bucket and shovel, hoping the horse would pooh outside their gate, they would then scoop it up to put it on the roses or rhubarb to help them grow.

This practice caused a few squabbles if the horse dared to pooh right between two gates, with each person declaring that pooh belonged to them.

Some of the horses had a weird kind of bag contraption attached to their rear end to catch their own pooh!

Once a month, the coal wagon would enter the quadrant, with the coalmen tipping a controlled amount of coal into the road outside people's houses. I wasn't too sure how it worked but it was entertaining to watch.

The driver would move slowly from one house to another, with the back of the lorry slightly tipped up, while a guy walked at the back pulling a lever that released the allocated amount of coal for each person. This procedure produced plumes of coal dust every time the coal hit the ground. No wonder the men looked so dirty.

Once the lorry left the estate, all the kids rushed indoors to get a metal bucket and a coal shovel, which was quite different from the usual shovel. The scoop part was broader with slightly rounded turned-up sides to shovel the coal more easily. Each family wanted to get their coal in before anyone else on the estate pinched it.

There was a precise procedure for this. The first task was to make sure the coal house door inside the kitchen had been firmly bolted shut. Then, armed with the metal bucket and two coal shovels, the girls would set about shovelling the coal into buckets. The boys would then carry the heavy buckets to the small trap-door in the back wall and tip the coal into the coal house. Once the last piece of coal was stored, the trap-door was bolted shut from the inside. While the coal was being transferred into the coal house, Audrey would position the tin bath in front of the open fire and boil the kettle to fill the bath.

Now it was time for the dirty coal boys and girls to get a quick dip in the little tin bath. It was such fun to bath in front of the fire instead of being in the big bath upstairs. The house was full of laughter. Once we were clean and dressed, the bath was carried by its handles to the back garden and the dirty water was poured onto the vegetable patch.

The streets on the estate were often dirty. Consequently, if we fell over and grazed our knees, within days the wound would start turning yellow and septic. If that happened to us, dad applied his special ingredients of mixed carbolic soap and sugar onto a piece of pink lint, which was then placed on the infected area and secured with a rag.

We used to visit an Aunty and Uncle who lived in The Avenue, a short walk from dad's house. Aunty Kit was my mother's sister and Uncle Tom her husband. They were very cheery people and always seemed pleased to see us.

I clearly remember the first time I met this aunty because I had never seen anyone with such enormous hips before. I thought she was a Crinoline Lady with a bustle under her skirt. My uncle wore special black boots. The left foot had a built up sole. He would laugh and tell us an elephant stood on his foot. Of course I believed his story. As a child I always believed what adults told me.

We also visited an aunty who lived across the road from dad's house. She was a more serious character of short stature. I never met an uncle there, but l think she had two daughters who were much older than me.

During subsequent visits while dad was at work down the pit, I was allowed to venture and explore further afield. There was only one rule. I had to be accompanied by one of my elder brothers or sisters.

We loved visiting the Miners' Welfare, which was about ten minutes' walk from the estate and stood in the centre of beautiful recreation grounds. It was a great place to play. There was a fantastic children's playing area with real swings, a teapot lid and a banana slide. We played there for hours, but if we got bored in the playground, we would wander off to the bowling green to watch the men, all smartly dressed in white, playing bowls, usually against another local team. We had to be very quiet if we watched them as they skimmed large wooden balls across the neatly mown green.

There was also a beautiful rose garden leading to the huge open plan green where we could run around, play ball games, chase each other and make as much noise as we wanted. These grounds were used by the local miners during their recreational time. The Backworth miners played many seasonal sports against opposing teams of miners from other pit villages. We often watched the men playing cricket.

When you entered the enormous sandstone-built Miners' Welfare Hall there were many rooms downstairs and a massive grand stairway in the centre of the hallway. The huge rooms downstairs were used for indoor activities.

One room housed two billiard tables with a rack fixed to the wall for the cues to stand in and bench seating against the wall with small tables in front for spectators. Another room had similar furnishing but with a couple of table tennis tables and dartboards. Of course, there was a large bar in each room for the men to buy beer and use the toilet facilities. Upstairs, there was a grand function room with a bar, with many tables and chairs around the walls. It also had a stage area, for the brass band to entertain the audience and, in the centre of the room there was a dance area.

We did not stay in that building very long because during the afternoons it was often full of men chatting and laughing and the rooms were frequently filled with the disgusting smell of cigarette smoke and beer.

We would continue walking through the grounds until we came to a set of double gates. Just across the main road from these gates, there was a cinema called the Backworth Gaff. My sister tells me it only cost about a shilling to see a movie and you could even get in for free if you handed in some jam jars for the manager's wife to use when she made her jam. On our way home we would call into the local Co-op corner shop and buy a half a pound of broken biscuits. If we smiled nicely, the shop keeper often gave us the packet free.

I have so many happy memories of the hours we played and explored in the park during my summer holiday home visits. Not the sound of a bell to be heard, beckoning us to return to the house for a meal. It was such a sense of freedom, to just play until we felt hungry enough to return to our house.

As a special treat, dad would let us go to the local 'Chippy' and buy a huge portion of chips with salt and vinegar and batter scraps. We would open the newspaper wrapping into the centre of the dining table and just eat from the paper to save the washing up. The chip supper was always accompanied by a drink of fizzy pop.

On the last evening before we returned to Hexham, during the summer holiday of 1958, there was a thunder and lightning storm. On one of those very rare occasions when the front door was open, Dad sat on one of those tiny three-legged stools in the doorway as we watched the sky light up with sheet lightning and listened to the rumble of the thunder. Dad said that, after the lightning, if I counted slowly until the sound of thunder came, that was the number of miles the centre of the storm was away from us. I snuggled up to dad as he hugged me when I was afraid of the noisy thunder.

I had no idea those moments would be the last I would share with him.

21

Your Dad is Dead

On Thursday 13th November 1958 I was told 'Your Dad is dead'.

I was 11 years old and it was my first term at the County Secondary School known to us as the senior school. I'd had a great day at school. My timetable meant I had attended all my favourite lessons, Domestic Science Maths, Music and General Science.

The Domestic Science lesson, which included doing needlecraft, was especially good that day because I was first in the class to finish making my PE gym skirt. That may not appear to be very important to some, but for me it was a great achievement because this meant I no longer had to wear well-worn washed out hand-me-down clothes. I could now wear my own hand-made skirt.

When I returned home after school, I followed the usual routine, of taking my outdoor coat off in the cloak room, making sure it was hung up in the correct place, and outdoor shoes were placed together in the cubby hole provided. I dashed upstairs and changed into playing-out clothes, not forgetting to neatly fold and place my school uniform on the bedside chair.

We usually played outside until the tea time bell rang out at 5-30pm, but on this particular day it had been raining and we had been ordered to play indoors. There were plenty of activities to occupy our time though. We could do homework, read a book or do some embroidery and, of course, there was always that 1000 piece jigsaw on the go!

I had chosen not to watch the small black and white television in the foyer. On that day the programme was Boots and Saddles, which pleased the boys as it was about the American Cavalry and Indians but it always seemed noisy and violent to me. I hated watching people fighting each other.

About 5pm, whispering started echoing through the house. Word was out that I had been summoned to the office. Fear ran through me. My experience of the office was that nobody went in there unless they were in trouble. A member of staff eventually came to collect me, she knocked on the office door, popped her head round the door and announced that I was present, reluctant to enter I was pushed from behind through the doorway.

It was a very small office with a window to the left of the doorway, two metal filing cabinets on the wall behind the door and a huge wooden desk with a very large typewriter in the centre of it. The Matron, or Superintendent as she was sometimes called, was sitting in a large office chair looking quite stern.

Surprisingly, she started talking in a more gentle voice than usual, but I have no recollection what was said until I heard the words. 'Your Dad is dead.'

With tears running down my cheeks I stared at her in disbelief, then, when she repeated those dreadful words, I knew it must be true.

Next thing I remember, was hearing the large metal bell positioned outside the office window, ringing to let everyone know it was time to come in for tea.

That was it! End of conversation!

There was no time to ask questions. Matron dismissed me from the office telling me not to be late for tea. I didn't get a chance to ask any of questions filling my mind.

Entering the dining room, I assumed that they had already been told why I had been in the office, because some of my friends also seemed to be upset.

I don't recall what was for tea, but I do remember feeling nauseous and not wanting to eat. However, not eating your meal was not an option. Thankfully, tea time was soon over and, as it was not my turn for clearing up duty, I asked if I could go to my dormitory to avoid being questioned by anyone.

I couldn't understand why my big sisters weren't there for me. My brothers were also missing. They had moved to the William Baker Technical College in London. Although we had spent some of our time living in different houses, their absence added to my upset, because they were like grown-ups to me and, one of them might have been able to answer my questions.

I felt there was no one I could talk to. When the other children came to bed at the normal bedtime, my friends in the dorm were really very kind to me, giving me hugs, telling me they were sorry my dad was dead and, some were crying with me. The after 'lights out' entertainment was cancelled that evening. Everyone went straight to sleep except for me of course.

It was horrid lying there, listening to the relaxed grunts and groans of the others sleeping. I just couldn't get to sleep because of all the questions still running through my head.

Why did he die? Had he been poorly? Had he been in an accident?

I had only just returned from my summer home visit. He seemed to be fine while I was there. Then I remembered he had been coughing a little more than usual and spitting into the fire. But I didn't think that was because he was unwell. He chewed tobacco or Bakki as he called it and, after a good chew, he'd spit remnants into the fire.

I kept asking myself if he had been unwell, why had I not noticed and, should I have noticed. Was I so excited about being at home that I just failed to notice?

I tried to convince myself they had made a dreadful mistake and got it wrong. It must be someone else's dad. Mine was fine last time I saw him.

I cried myself to sleep but kept waking up thinking it was just nasty dream. Everyone else was asleep. There was nobody to talk to.

I wanted to ask a member of staff if what I had been told earlier was true, but I didn't dare venture out onto the landing, there were dire consequences for breaking rules. Standing at the stair-head freezing, was the last thing I needed.

Feeling I had only just managed to fall asleep and that I had been awake most of the night, I was woken up by the member of staff on wake up duty, barging her way through the door shouting, 'Morning girls,' as she marched down the centre of the dorm pulling our bedding off. I felt dreadful and was still feeling very tired. I found it difficult to drag myself out of bed.

No one asked how I was or, if I was feeling okay to go to school. The rule was, unless you had a high temperature or you were covered in spots, you went to school and, as I had neither of those, off to school it was.

Most of that morning is a blur. I expect I ate some breakfast before setting off on the long walk to school. I don't think I attended many lessons that day. I was unable to concentrate and was taken to the staff room. Whilst there, I realised that I had stopped crying about my dad being dead. My thoughts had switched to thinking that if it's true he is dead, would I still be able visit dad's house next summer. And, if we did go home, who would look after us.

One of the teachers asked me if I was going to my father's funeral. I can still picture the look of shock on her face when I replied 'What's a funeral?' She explained it was when the family get together to say goodbye to someone who had died.

On reflection, I expect children were considered to be too young to attend funerals. At just eleven years old, I certainly had no idea what happened to people when they died.

Once back at the orphanage, I took the risk and dared to ask a member of staff. 'How do you know my dad is dead?'

She replied, 'The Superintendent had received a phone call from a relative.'

Then she told me not to question what I had been told. 'Facts are facts.'

Somehow I managed to survive the rest of the day and managed to have a better sleep, despite my head still being full of unanswered questions.

There was no escape from Saturday morning duties they still had to be done. After lunch I decided not to visit town. While most of the other children were out and, after great deliberation, I plucked up the courage to ask that same member of staff I had spoken to on Friday evening, if I was suffering from 'mourning' sickness. She just laughed at me, saying, 'Of course not.'

'You can only have 'morning sickness' if you are having a baby.' Her laughter and comments really upset and confused me. Why was she laughing and talking about having a baby?

At eleven years old I had no idea about having babies, but I had heard the term 'morning sickness' before. I was being serious. I really thought my crying was due to me 'mourning' the loss of my dad.

I also dared to ask, 'Why had God taken my dad to Heaven when he already had my Mother?' and told the member of staff that, 'it just wasn't fair.'

She was furious and replied that I should be grateful my father was dead, because, some children at the orphanage had fathers who were still alive but didn't want them. I was told to stop feeling sorry for myself and think about how they must feel.

Until that moment, it had never entered my head to question why the other children were in the home. I just thought we were all orphans. I was totally unaware that some of the other children could have been unwanted kids.

None of the questions I asked were answered to my satisfaction.

That whole episode shattered my perception of life.

My final home visit:

I had wanted to return home the following summer because although nine months had passed since we had been told dad was dead, I still couldn't believe it and, I wanted to see for myself that he wasn't there anymore. However the general consensus seemed to be that we should not be allowed to return home. I don't recall being asked by anyone if I wanted to go back home but, I do remember saying I wanted to go home for my summer holiday.

My records reveal: There was great deliberation and communication between the Superintendent and Headquarters. *After an inspection of the family home it was decided that I could return, providing Audrey was available to look after and supervise me. Thankfully she did return to look after us.*

The atmosphere of the house had changed. The visit proved to be a very difficult time for me, as I struggled, to come to terms with dad's absence.

Now, still just twelve years old, I found it very difficult to understand my emotions. It even crossed my mind that my dad, might have been like other dads of children in the orphanage I had been told about, who had decided that they didn't want to be a dad anymore. I had only known my dad during those three summer home visits and had just got used to the idea of having a dad.

I was still waiting for someone to answer the question I had asked nine months earlier. I tried playing on the green with the other kids, and even ventured to our favourite park, but I kept spoiling the fun by asking if we could go home. I could see Audrey was upset herself, so I didn't think she would want me blubbering on at her, with those same questions still locked inside my head.

There was one occasion when I was sitting with friends on the green, I told them that I was going back to our house, but, when Audrey went to the green looking for me I wasn't there. My friends told Audrey I said 'I was going home.

Apparently, this caused quite a panic with all the neighbours asking each other if they had seen me. I was eventually found sitting on the wall at the bus stop. Everyone was shouting at me. I hadn't realised my actions would cause such a commotion. I'd just wanted to sit on the wall waiting for dad to get off the pit bus as he used to. But he never did.

Probably because I was upsetting the others, I was sent back to Hexham and never went to the family home again.

Years later, I returned to find the quadrant of houses had been demolished.

22

Christmas Preparations

For me, the Christmas festivities began the first weekend of December when the students from the 'Hydro' arrived to help us make coloured paper chains to decorate the houses. We were given large sheets of paper; red, green, blue or yellow. Our first task was to take one sheet of paper and, using a pencil and a twelve inch wooden ruler, measure and draw an oblong 2" by 6" as many times as we could, then laboriously cut out each individual strip. As you can imagine, this method of preparation took hours to complete.

Then, one year, a new student showed us how to fold the paper over few times before cutting, which enabled us to cut out several strips at a time and reduce the cutting stage. Once cut, the strips were stacked into piles of separate colours.

We then selected one colour from each pile and glued each end of a strip, making a circle, then, interlocking a different colour each time until we had created a beautiful paper chain about a yard long. As they were completed, we laid the chains out on the playing room floor to dry.

Once they had dried, a long loop of wool was attached to each end. At the end of the day, all the chains were gently placed into a box and put into storage.

While we were making chains, a second of group of children was given small squares of shiny red, silver, gold or green card to cut into festive shapes baubles, bells or holly leaves. They were used to make special 'Thank You' Christmas cards for the various groups of people who had donated clothes or gifts to the orphanage throughout the year.

On the last Friday of term a huge Christmas tree, kindly donated by one of our sponsors appeared in the hallway. That was it, the signal Christmas was really here. That same evening, children of all age groups were given the opportunity to help adorn the tree.

I remember, in my early years, there was a battered fairy positioned at the very top of the tree, but, alas she finally disintegrated and was replaced by a large shiny star. Once the centre piece was in place, the taller children started placing tinsel and hanging festive objects on the upper branches of the tree, leaving the lower branches free for the shorter, younger children.

The chains we had made earlier were retrieved from storage, then, we were given the okay to decorate the house. A senior child stood on a chair to reach up and slip the wool loops on the chain, over the top corners of every door downstairs and onto all the windows in the ballroom.

If there were any of the shiny bells, baubles or holly leaves left, we used wool to attach them to the chains hanging at the ballroom windows. These simple colourful paper chains made the home look bright and Christmassy.

On Party days, a buzz of excitement filled the air. Once lunch was finished and the routine household chores were hastily done, we anxiously waited for the member of staff to carry out the inspection, hoping we wouldn't have to redo anything. Nod given, we raced upstairs and waited to be allocated the party frock we would wear for all the Christmas parties to be held during that particular festive season.

The girls living in the Cottage and the bungalow joined us on the landing for the distribution of party dresses. As we eagerly waited for the member staff to make her entrance, we sat cross-legged, staring into the open cupboard at all those beautiful shiny satin or lace party dresses, pointing at dresses that were not in the wardrobe last year and hoping we would get the chance to wear our favourite choice of dress that someone had worn the Christmas before.

There was an occasion I had to wait for two years to wear the beautiful dress my sister had previously worn. Everyone immediately fell silent when the member of staff entered the landing area. She would reach for a dress, hold it up in front of us all as she weighed up the size of it before handing it to the child she thought it would fit.

The silence was never broken, but if she held up the dress we hoped would be ours, we would give our broadest smiles, sit there bolt upright with our chests thrust forward like proud peacocks, shouting 'Me, me, me!' inside our heads. All the party dresses were so beautiful and colourful, I never minded too much if I wasn't given the one I liked best.

I always seemed to get a dress meant for someone carrying more weight than me, though, thankfully most dresses had sashes in those days, so I just fastened my sash a little tighter around my waist to reduce the bagginess. Then I would spin and dance around, feeling like a princess. I don't expect there was as much fuss in the boys' dormitory. They just wore their Sunday short navy trousers and a shirt and tie.

During mid-afternoon a bus load of ladies would arrive from one of the many distant Women's Institutes which had donated unwanted clothes and toys to the orphanage throughout the year. We entertained them to say 'Thank you' for all their kindness. We lined up in the hallway to greet the visitors and as instructed, we'd smile and give a semi curtsy as they entered the front door.

As the ladies approached, we would politely say 'hello' and ask them if they would like to be shown around the house. Without hesitation, they always replied 'Oh yes, please.' So off we went in little groups, first to show them where the downstairs cloakroom was, so they could hang up their coats and be aware of the location of the toilet facilities. Then we headed upstairs to show them our very tidy dormitories and the bathroom.

They generally asked questions like 'Do you all get on together in the same bedroom?' and 'Are you able to sleep in the same room as your sisters or cousins?' We explained that the sleeping arrangements were determined by age groups and we felt that we were all sisters anyway.

Returning downstairs we continued the tour by showing them the dining room, which prompted questions 'What's the food like?' and 'Are you fed well?' We didn't dare reply with a derogatory comment.

Not all the children liked having strangers in the house. A few of them felt they were just being gawped at and hated the visitors asking too many questions.

'How long have you lived here?' 'Is it nice living here?' And 'Are the staff kind to you?'

Even worse, was being told you were wearing a dress they had donated. I was used to their questioning so it never bothered me.

When the mealtime hand bell rang out, we escorted our guests to the dining room which was looking very Christmassy and colourful. Some of the small dining tables had been pushed together and placed inside the square bay window and covered with a white cotton bed sheet.

The table was set out with an appetizing buffet prepared by cook with the help of the senior girls. There were neatly cut triangular sandwiches with a variety of fillings, usually egg, paste or spam. Also on offer, cheese finger scones, fruit scones, sweet mince pies, slices of jam Swiss roll and chocolate Yuletide logs.

We invited our guests to collect paper napkins and side plates from a small occasional table and to select some food, before escorting them to one of the chairs placed in rows around the room. The older girls were responsible for offering the ladies a cup of tea.

Once all the ladies were settled into a seat with their plate of food and cup of tea, we were then given the customary nod that it was now our turn to collect a plate and select a small quantity of food before returning to our seat.

Earlier that afternoon we had been warned not to be greedy by putting too much food on our plates. The food was for the guests. We could eat the leftovers after our visitors had gone home, though.

Another nod from staff indicated that all the guests had finished eating. We collected the dirty dishes and stacked then into the hatch for the older girls doing the washing up.

We escorted the ladies through the hallway, past the guest cloakroom and into the ballroom, where chairs had been strategically placed around the walls.

We were expected to chat to the visitors until the older girls arrived after finishing their washing up chores. When the senior girls joined us, it was time for the entertainment to begin.

As a member of staff started to crank the handle of the gramophone we grabbed our partner and assembled ourselves in a line, ready for take-off.

I don't recall any arguments over who would get a chance to dance with the boys. I was too young to be interested in them and, after all, they were just somebody's brothers. Besides boys at the orphanage were well outnumbered by girls during the early 1950's, so girls just danced with girls.

Our well-rehearsed exhibition dances always started with the Grand Old Duke of York. We set off galloping up and down in time to the music, singing along as we danced.

Our enthusiasm for dancing always generated great laughter from ourselves and the visitors, we giggled so much as we danced to the tempo of the ever changing beat of the music. Other dances included the Cumberland Square Eight, the Gay Gordon, the Waltz and the Quick Step.

The atmosphere toned down when we embarrassingly had to approach our guests and ask if they would like to be our partner for the last waltz. That in itself was extraordinary, because it was the one and only time of the year that we actually had close physical contact with adults. We lived in a world of no outstretched arms of comfort or cuddles. So, it was a very strange experience for us to be held up close to an actual adult human body.

Just imagine where my face was being squeezed towards when I was aged between five and ten years old. I can tell you, it was usually in the region between their waist, or bustline. The odour coming from these ladies was strange, bodily and perfumed odours I had never encountered before. I now recognise those smells to be general body odour, and stale cigarette smoke.

We probably smelled a bit strange too because we always washed with Carbolic soap! Needless to say I was relieved when the record had finished and the waltzing came to a halt.

We could never be classed as a choir, but, when the dancing was finished and we had ushered our dancing partners back to their seats, we bunched together and sang heartily.

'We wish you a Merry Christmas, We wish you a Merry Christmas,
We wish you a Merry Christmas and a Happy New Year.'

After polite applause from the guests, that was it, party over. The president of the group would then give her little speech to thank us very much for inviting them to the party, stating how much they had enjoyed our entertainment. Adding how lucky we were to live in such a beautiful house and have such lovely ladies looking after us, etc. etc.

Speech over, we then escorted the ladies to the cloakroom to collect their coats and left them to chat among themselves and use the toilet facilities if required. Still chatting, they returned to the hallway wearing their coats ready for the journey home. After a few more hugs and squeezes to say good bye, they set off toward their waiting bus.

As instructed we crammed into the circular vestibule at the front door to wave good bye as the bus disappeared down the driveway.

23

Christmas Time

Decorating the Christmas tree was definitely the signal our extensive, noisy and excitable Christmas festivities were about to begin. Looking back, I accept it must have been a very difficult time for the member of staff on duty in the main house to cope with twenty or so highly strung children, especially on Christmas Eve.

We did try to follow the normal daily routine. Wakeup call and breakfast were at the usual times, and the basic house duties still had to be done. If Christmas Eve was on Sunday, we still attended the Abbey morning service and Sunday school but we didn't have to attend the evening service.

We laughed, sang and played our way through the day. It was the one and only time the Sunday rule, to be respectably quiet all day, was broken.

After our evening meal, there was no problem persuading us it was time for bed. We would race upstairs, follow the bath-time routine by getting into our nightwear as soon as we could, knowing we would then be able to collect a pillowcase from the cupboard shelf on the landing and return to the dining room. We turned the pillowcase inside out so the inside fold could loop over the back of our chair and we excitedly chatted about what we might find in the morning.

The staff knew which chair each child occupied so that made it much easier for them to ensure the boys didn't get gifts meant for the girls or vice-versa.

During my time at the orphanage, I don't recall seeing any adverts on television to show children the latest toys, dolls or games in the shops, so the expectations of the children then, was totally different to the demands of children today.

As a child, I had no knowledge or understanding of the concept of Father Christmas or Santa Claus. Yes, I had seen a man dressed up and giving children presents, but I had no idea he was regarded as a traditional figure.

We were very grateful for all our donated gifts and had no idea in advance what we might receive, although we always knew in the bottom of the pillowcase we would find a tangerine or apple and, a big brown one penny.

After our hot cocoa and a prolonged chatter about what we might get, it was time to head up the stairs for bed and try a little harder than usual to get to sleep. Occasionally, we actually escaped hearing Evil Edna saying. 'If you don't behave yourself, you won't get any Christmas presents. So you won't.' I'm so relieved I can now laugh at the memory of her ranting on.

Needless to say, there was absolutely no chance that we would be going straight to sleep. In fact, I'm quite sure the dorm entertainment was extended.

Thankfully, I have no recollection of anyone from my dorm, doing the gruelling landing punishment on Christmas Eve.

On Christmas morning, we were not allowed to rush downstairs to see what was in our pillowcases. As usual, we had to wait for our wakeup call before we could get up.

Eventually, a jovial member of staff would enter the dorm saying 'Merry Christmas, girls,' and in return we would chant, 'Merry Christmas Miss.'

This was the one and only day she made her way down the centre of the dormitory to open the curtains and windows without pulling our bedding off as she passed by. We hastily went through the morning routine, omitting house duties because today was the cleaners, or should I say 'our,' day off. We still had to make our beds though. Only then, could we rush downstairs to see our presents.

I remember one particular year there was absolute mayhem in the dining room because we were supposed to collect our by now bulging pillowcases and take them to the play room before we looked through them.

Some new arrivals, experiencing their first Christmas with us, were not aware of all the house rules so they were excitedly rummaging through their goodies. But, with guidance from the older children, they bundled their presents back into the pillowcases and headed towards the playroom area.

We only had a short time to look at our gifts before the bell rang out for breakfast.

Although the gifts were our own, they were rarely solely for the individual recipient. Until the late 50's, the pillowcases were filled with toys for sharing, such as jigsaws, board games and playing cards etc.

That said, we were delighted with our presents because, by now, most of last year's games were well worn out or had pieces missing. The younger girls were given new dolls or teddies, while the boys received cars or tractors. Older girls were restocked with sewing and knitting paraphernalia.

I have absolutely no idea what gifts the older boys aged between ten and fourteen received. By the 1960's, more thought was given to what may suit the individual child, for example bath cubes or talcum powder for the girls.

Breakfast was set out and presented as any normal day. There was no point rushing our breakfast to make an early escape to play with our presents. Our strict rules meant, even on Christmas day, we had to wait for everyone to finish eating before we could be excused from the dining room. Alas, there was no escape from dining room or washing up duty, they still had to be done.

After breakfast the youngsters settled into one of the playrooms to play with their new toys, while the senior children (11-14 year olds) had to sort themselves out for the long walk to Hexham for the Christmas morning service at the Abbey. I loved those joyous services and always sang my heart out.

The cook always rustled up a delicious Christmas lunch with all the trimmings. The tables were set out using the best china with the vegetables presented in tureens. 'Afters' was always Christmas pudding, with a surprise inside, served with white sauce.

It took me years to work out how everyone managed to get a silver sixpence wrapped with grease proof paper inside their Christmas pudding. Eventually, I discovered that the sixpence was discreetly placed into each portion as it was being served onto the dish.

I have absolutely no idea if the children from the Cottage and Bungalow came to the main house to join us so we could have the festive lunch together. However, I do remember all the children definitely joined in the ballroom party time during the afternoon and evening.

After lunch, the girls dashed straight upstairs to change out of our Sunday best clothes into our treasured party frocks. I always considered my party dresses to be very precious, especially the beautifully made pink chiffon dress my sister had previously worn.

The boys probably just stayed in their Sunday smart clothes. I can't visualise them in special party clothes. Perhaps, I just wasn't interested enough to notice what they were wearing!

Once everyone was accounted for in the ballroom, the old gramophone was cranked up in readiness for us to start dancing to the music of the Gay Gordon, the Eightsome Reel and the Grand Old Duke of York. We galloped around with such enthusiasm and gusto.

We then played Musical Chairs, Pass the Parcel and Blind Man's bluff, which must have been a hilarious game for the spectators to watch. One person was blindfolded and had to guess the identity of the person who had been placed in front of them by fumbling around and asking questions. It was a fun game which could be quite embarrassing at times, particularly if you failed to name your best friend or a sibling.

We must have stopped the party antics at some point to have tea in the dining room because I can't imagine us having tea set out in the ball room. That was a strictly no food and drink area during the early to late-fifties. There was a lovely spread for tea, triangle meat paste or egg sandwiches, a selection of small cakes, jelly and custard trifle then finishing with a piece of homemade Christmas cake.

The strict rules on table manners still applied. You were not allowed to take a cake until after you had eaten at least one sandwich and you could not go back to have another sandwich after you had eaten cake.

Even at party time there was always the fear of being watched and punished for breaking the table manners rules.

I'm not sure if the regular bedtimes were extended on Christmas Day, but I do recall the groans filling the air when a member of staff declared it was bedtime for the younger children. That declaration was always followed by a prolonged hugging for the children about to be dispatched to their own houses, because that was it party over. The individual staff member took her children back to the cottage then the older children had to make sure the ballroom was left clean and tidy, before their member of staff took them back to the bungalow.

We carefully hung our party dresses back in the landing cupboard until we needed them for the next party. Presumably, we had our quick bath in the customary finger depth of water, and cleaned our teeth before getting into our flannelette nightdresses. Then, kneeling by our beds, we thanked Jesus for our lovely Christmas presents and for blessing us with such a very happy day.

Of course, we still broke the rules by having our after lights out entertainment!

Regrettably, I can't recall all the names of all our generous sponsors, and the companies who kindly organised parties for us during the Christmas holidays.

I do remember Carrs Biscuits of Carlisle, Clarks Shoes in Kendal, Rowntree's factory in York, British Ropes Wallsend, and the men from a working men's club in Prudhoe who called themselves, 'The Jolly Boys.' I particularly remember going to the Rowntree's sweet factory because it was the furthest distance we travelled from Hexham, and, we were given the most sweets!

At least two members of staff travelled with us on the bus trips to the parties. We had a repertoire of songs to sing during what seemed to be very long distance journeys to and from our destinations. 'She'll be coming round the mountain,' 'It's a long way to Tipperary,' 'Old McDonald had a farm,' 'Ten green bottles,' and 'If you're happy and you know it clap your hands' to name a few. Our singing also worked as a method of distraction for the children who were likely to suffer from travel sickness. Sickness was more prevalent on the homeward journey though, probably due to the over indulgence at the party!

The format of the parties, which were held in the factory staff canteen, was pretty much the same at all the venues. There was always a meet and greet reception, then we hung our Burberrys in the cloakroom and were advised to use the toilet facilities before being shown into the party area where we played musical chairs and other festive games. Then we were seated at long trestle tables decorated with Christmas logs and holly.

We wore the party hats from inside the Christmas crackers and tucked into the delicious party spread. When we had just about eaten everything in sight, a guy dressed in a Santa Claus outfit handed out presents to everyone.

When party time was over, we were rounded up to dutifully thank the men dressed in smart suits assembled in the canteen, by singing what had become our traditional thank you song, 'We wish you a Merry Christmas and a Happy New Year.'

We collected our Burberrys to the echo of 'Have you been?' resounding through the cloakroom. Once we were all accounted for, we clambered onto the bus ready for the homeward journey, and vigorously waved goodbye to our hosts as we left.

Only as an adult, have I realised how difficult it must have been for the poor driver to concentrate on his driving with a group of giddy, loudly singing children on board his bus. Not forgetting the smelly mess made by the children who didn't quite reach the bucket before being sick.

I remember my Christmas festivities being full of laughter and happy times.

24

Beyond the Walls

Employment options for girls were very limited when I left the orphanage, although the advantages of being a mother's help or housekeeper were not apparent to me then, but I know now the greatest benefit was to ensure we had a roof over our heads. I remember being asked if I would like to be a housekeeper or look after children. Without hesitation my reply was to look after children, because at that particular time I felt I had been a domestic cleaner from the age of seven and visualised that being a housekeeper meant doing domestic chores every day of the week, or even the rest of my life.

Of course, the girls who had lived in the bungalow for the past two years, were given plenty of reminders that they were preparing to venture into the outside world, but the first indication a room-mates departure was imminent, came when they were presented with a copy of the Bible and a suitcase to pack their smart Saturday and Sunday clothes. There were no farewell parties, the girls not about to leave went to school as normal each day not knowing if their friend or room-mate would still be in the bungalow on their return.

I particularly found the period immediately after I was told to pack my case was a very traumatic time. Despite being warned in advance that preparations were being made for me to leave the orphanage I had called my home for the past twelve years. There were lots of tears and hugs with long-term friends.

We had shared our rollercoaster life together and had built such a bond over the years that we were like sisters. We had endured a harsh regime but were now enjoying a more relaxed culture, implemented by the new superintendent.

My Correspondence and Visitors record shows that in the weeks before I left, my sister June visited me for two separate overnight stays during February and March and also that my two brothers and my sister May had written to me. Probably to reassure me that all would be well and I would survive beyond the walls just as they had. My records also revealed that I left the orphanage during May 1963.

I have no memory of my actual departure, or how I arrived at my destination in Gosforth where I was to be employed as a mother's help. Presumably I had met the couple and their two children prior to being employed by them but I have no recollection of being introduced to them before I arrived on their doorstep.

They were a very nice professional couple living in a luxurious home. As they already had a cleaner/housekeeper working for them, my tasks were purely related to looking after the two young school aged boys, getting them ready for school and having breakfast with them before one of the parents drove them to a local private school.

During the morning, my job was to return the toys they had been playing with to the playroom, make their beds and give anywhere the boys had been a quick tidy up. Jobs done, I was free to stroll around the local park or window shop on the high street until mid-afternoon when they returned from school.

Once the boys returned, I gave them a light snack then I would occupy them in their garden or play room until the housekeeper had prepared the evening meal. After bathing and preparing the boys for bed, I handed them over to their parents, who by this time had returned from work. My duties were usually finished by 6pm.

I then retired to my own posh bedroom with a television and a bed with the deepest mattress I had seen in my life. I was living a life of luxury, having three square meals a day and receiving £3:00 per week pocket money. So why was I so unhappy and crying myself to sleep at night? I wasn't prepared for the silence and sense of isolation. I felt traumatised. This lifestyle was totally alien to me. It wasn't just my friends I was missing. It was the whole structure and routine of life I had become accustomed to that I was missing the most. You may think I would be relieved not to have someone telling me when to wake up and when to go to bed, but I was not.

At no time had I practiced using an alarm clock, and had never thought about how long it would take me to get dressed and be prepared for work in the morning. For the past sixteen years that had been done for me. I didn't miss queuing up to use the toilet though.

I cried myself to sleep most nights because I missed chatting with my room-mates, and when the alarm clock rang out to waken me in the morning, I felt dreadful and did not want to get out of bed. However being with the lovely, well-behaved, smiling boys was just what I needed in the mornings to cheer me up and besides, I had learned at a very early age how to disguise my emotions.

Having too much time to think about missing my friends during my off duty period was my biggest problem. After a very short while, I realised that I was entrapped in my luxurious room and became bored with watching too much television.

Being idle for hours was alien to me, and I was really missing my soul mates. Even meeting up with new found friends at the church youth club didn't console me. I know it must seem surprising to some but, when I left Barnardo's at sixteen years old I had never been to a supermarket or a clothes shop. Our clothes came out of a cupboard. I remember being amazed the first time I went into a grocery store. I couldn't believe how small tins of beans were or how other food products were packed because I was used to seeing everything in catering tins.

Gosforth was a lovely location, but I was afraid to venture out into a strange environment alone. When I did go out I frequently felt anxious and panicked in case I had strayed too far from the house and couldn't find my way back.

My brothers lived miles away in London and, although I knew the addresses where my sisters lived, finding them by using public transport was beyond my comprehension. I had never planned a journey on my own before.

A Barnardo's aftercare worker came to visit me. I assumed that was because I had been in my employment for six months. During our conversation, it soon became apparent I was upset when I blurted out all the emotions bottled up inside me. I found it very difficult to explain why I was so unhappy without sounding ungrateful to the couple who had kindly opened their door to me. The care-worker seemed to understand the reason why I was unsettled. Presumably after discussions and deliberation about the reasons I was struggling to cope with life beyond those walls, the decision was made that I could move on and be relocated.

I had my very first interview for a job to work in a shop, where I would have an opportunity to communicate with people and hopefully feel less isolated. So in December 1963, lodgings were found for me with a family living in Benwell, Newcastle, and I began my new employment as a shop assistant in a small department store located on Westgate Road, just a short walking distance from my lodgings.

I loved that job. The Manager and the other assistants were very kind and supportive. I had no problem getting myself to work on time and, enjoyed chatting to the customers and my work colleagues. They showed me where to catch a (Wrights bus?) to Hexham so I could visit aunty Jo and uncle Ken who were still running Mount Royal. I enjoyed and needed to return to the place I had called home for twelve years.

Alas, the situation at my lodgings was becoming more unsettled. The couple and their grown up sons were lovely and made me feel so welcome but, I was afraid of being the only girl in the house. Nobody threatened or harmed me, but I couldn't cope with my own inner fears of having to use a mixed gender bathroom, especially after living for years with all male areas being 'no go' zones.

We sat at a table and ate all our meals together, then chatted as we squeezed onto the sofa to watch television in the evening and I was comfortable and happy with that, but, when it was bedtime I became unsettled, because there were no rules set out about the use of the bathroom. I found it very confusing when I found the bathroom door closed because I could never tell if it was occupied or not. All was well if I was first upstairs for bed. I used the bathroom before going to my room, but once I was ready for bed, I was afraid to venture out of my room. I was even too scared to knock on the bathroom door because I became embarrassed if someone was already in there. Some nights, I lay in bed for ages wondering if I dare go to the toilet.

I have no recollection of the reasons why I had to leave my lodgings after being there for five months. My memories of living with the family in Benwell are happy ones apart from my stupid fear of using a shared bathroom, However, My records reveal that my behaviour was becoming too difficult for my landlady to cope with, but, also stated that the home situation was unsettled and there were financial issues.

During May 1964, I was found new lodgings in an area called Holy Cross, Wallsend. My dear landlady, Mrs Sloan, was the most supportive and understanding person I had met since leaving the Orphanage. The arrangement suited both of us. She was a widow with one child who had recently married and left home, she needed company and I wanted a place to call home.

I was totally spoilt while I lived there. For the first time ever in my life, I was woken up every morning with a cup of tea delivered to my bedroom. Once dressed and downstairs, there was a cooked breakfast waiting for me and a sandwich for my lunchtime break at the store where I still worked. I now travelled to my workplace in Newcastle by bus.

The community spirit on the estate was similar to that of Backworth where my dad had lived. Everyone seemed to look out for each other and they were very helpful and friendly. There were two families with teenage children who lived in the next street to me. We became very good friends and I joined in with their outdoor activities. Basically we just messed about in the street, playing ball games or skipping. On rainy days we took turns to gather in one of the houses, and listened to records on a record player that didn't need winding up!

Although my friends were always welcome to visit me at my lodgings, they occasionally grumbled when they were sent home at 8pm because they were allowed out until later. They were surprised to find I lived by curfew rules, which meant I must be home by 8pm if I was at work the next day or back in the house by 9pm on any other evening. I was very happy to have boundaries and structure in place again.

When the boys became old enough to have scooters, they rode them around the estate without wearing headgear. I presume this was until they needed a licence or had to pass some sort of driving test when they would be able to venture beyond the estate. Being a pillion passenger for the first time terrified me, much to the amusement of my friends. I screamed and clung on for dear life, but I soon enjoyed the excitement of tearing around the estate. At some point we joined the local scooter club and ventured far and wide. I was having the time of my life.

Reluctantly my relationship with Uncle Mac had continued after I left the orphanage. I still wrote to him but made excuses such as having to work, in an attempt to avoid going on holiday with him. I also manage to persuade him not to visit me at my lodgings. I was still afraid to stop all contact with him for fear I would be considered ungrateful for all the lovely gifts he had given me.

Eventually I gave in to his requests and joined him for a week in Folkestone, taking one of my new found friends with me. During the holiday I mentioned that I had joined the scooter club with male and female friends and, that I was enjoying the happiest phase of my teenage years. I thought he was pleased that I was happy. He actually offered to buy me a scooter.

Within a week of returning to my lodgings, I received a letter from him that truly shocked me. He rambled on about the type of life I was leading and, quoted the words of a popular song at that time. 'You always hurt the one you love.' I decided to share my anxieties with my works' Manager. He realised how shocked I was and advised me to discuss the letter with an after-care worker.

My Boss telephoned Barnardo's Regional Office in Jesmond, informing them of the situation. That same day an after-care worker arrived to see me. At last, I finally met someone I dared to share my inner fears with.

He listened intently as I poured out the saga of my anxiety and concerns associated with my tenuous relationship with Uncle Mac during the preceding years. He read the letter then, took possession of the letter and advised me not to reply or, worry about the situation anymore, the matter would be dealt with. Thankfully, within a few days I received a letter from Barnardo's Head Office, confirming that the relationship should be terminated immediately. I never heard from Uncle Mac again.

My intention is not to be disrespectful to this, now deceased man, who appeared to be a kind hearted gentleman. But, to this day, I cannot understand why anyone, even back in the 1950's and 60's could think that a sixty-plus year old bachelor, who lived more than three hundred miles away, would be a suitable companion to a vulnerable ten year old girl.

I'm not sure if the above events caused added concerns about my welfare but, I became aware that after-care workers were trying to negotiate with my eldest brother and, legal guardian, to accept responsibility for me before my eighteenth birthday when I would no longer be the responsibility of Barnardo's.

The idea of living with my brother scared me, because I didn't even know him.

The first few months of 1965, was an extraordinary time for me. I was encouraged to leave my employment and my friends at the store, to work in a factory situated on the Coast Road, Wallsend, just across the road from where my brother Bob lived.

I'm not sure of the sequence of events but, at some point I was reintroduced to my brother. That was a very scary experience for me. I tried to make sense of meeting this guy I knew very little about and, being told this is your eldest brother.

I didn't even recognise him, because I hadn't had any contact with him since before the death of my Dad, seven years earlier. Yet this thirty-four year old stranger was my legal guardian and, I was going to be relocated to live with him, his wife and daughter.

I was an emotional wreck by the time I moved out of my lodgings. I had to leave people I had become attached to, my dearest Mrs Sloan and my friends. I was now reliving the trauma of leaving my friends at the orphanage.

Fortunately, my brother lived less than a mile away from my friends so I was able to continue my relationship with them and visit them as often as I could.

I soon adjusted to life with Bob and living with him was not as bad as I had expected. My new job gave me the opportunity to meet lots of new friends who persuaded me to join the Works' Athletics Club, where I could return to my love of running. The club was also a venue for social evenings at weekends with visiting rock bands.

That was a great era for me, rocking and rolling the night away with friends although I did have to be back in the house by a 10pm deadline.

While living with Bob, he told me that Dad had been making financial contributions toward our up keep, while we were in the care of Barnardo's, until the day he died. Then, after Dad's death in November 1958, Bob continued the payments, with money paid to him, by the Coal Miners Pension Scheme. I found this information very hard to believe, because I had never heard about that happening before.

Bob convinced me this information was true, by showing me the actual receipts he had kept as proof of payment. The first in his possession was dated December 1949 and others dated up to 1961. Although my archive records show that payments were made up to July 1963.

I continued visiting my friends on the estate and enjoyed having lots of fun with new found friends at the George Angus factory, all in-all I was happy and content.

I don't recall any significant build-up to my imminent closure with Barnardo's but I am now aware that on my 18th Birthday, 30th March 1965, I was 'Written Off.'

Copy of maintenance receipt.

Barnardo's summary of my life.

25

Tribute to my Dad
Jacob Thompson
1909-1958

It upset me to discover in my notes that it was suggested my dad could make a contribution toward his five children if they were accepted by Barnardo's because in someone's opinion, he spent too much time and money womanising at the local club. The judgement made that he should pay ten shilling a week for each child was nearly a third of his £7 per week wage. I believe the penalty for having a drink with his mates and taking the opportunity to ask ladies for advice on how to cope with ten children on his own was a perfectly legitimate thing to do, and the penalty he paid was a disproportionate price to pay for his crime. Especially as my eldest brother Bob told me dad had struggled until his dying day to maintain the payments because he still had to pay his rent and provide for the children staying at home.

Although I only knew my dad for three, two week, summer holiday home visits, reading through my archive notes made me realise that dad had done the best he could for all my family under the tragic circumstances he found himself in after the death of our mother. When the five youngest children were placed in an orphanage in Scotland he wanted us back in England so he could visit occasionally. Then when we did return to England but in single gender homes, he wanted us to be together. I also believe he instigated my return from being fostered, again because he wanted to stay in contact with me and keep the youngest of his family together.

RIP.
Dad you were much loved and appreciated

26

Reflections

Although I'm pleased with my decision to retrieve my archived notes, I have to admit I am still shocked by the revelations about my being boarded out and having to accept the logged events are actually about me. Thank goodness I have no memory of that episode. I was disappointed to find crucial records covering the period of my father's death are missing from my archive notes.

I decided to write this book to enlighten my grandchildren about what life was like for a child living in an Orphanage during the 1950's. And to accentuate the progress that has been made to improve the welfare of children in care today.

I encountered difficulty writing some aspects of my past, especially those relating to my lack of support, immediately after the death of my dad during November 1958 which was my most traumatic episode. However, I find it reassuring to know that such a scenario is less likely to happen today.

Despite living within a very strict regime, my pre-dominant memories of life in the orphanage are those of great friendships and happy times full of laughter. Overall I have survived unscathed, other than a few compulsive behaviours, such as having to fold all items of clothing in a precise way, spooning all the cutlery together and having all tinned produce with their labels facing to the front. And, folding all paper wrappers and tying them in a knot before placing them in the bin.

I became aware my behaviours were different to that of others whilst attending a works training session headed; Understanding Autism. I realised that I had at least 75% of similarities for the same behaviours, much to the amusement of my work colleagues and myself. That was when I realised not everyone needs to do things quite the same as me.

Prior to my retirement I enjoyed a most rewarding thirty year career, working within various aspects of residential childcare. During that time, I witnessed and worked through many changes for the better relating to the care of children, including the realisation that looking after children involves not only looking after their physical needs alone.

Carers now strive to put more emphasis on children's emotional needs by, listening to their views, with the overriding principle that, 'Every Child Matters'.

I was destined to follow a career in childcare because I strongly believe all children should be treated as individuals and, as an adult I realised the consequences had I been left at home with my dad.

It was also my way to express my appreciation for being cared for by Barnardo's.

My employment experiences have given me a greater understanding of the drawbacks faced by childcare staff. I can now empathise with and, have great respect for the staff who dedicated their lives to ensure my childhood was the best it could have been.

Friends have spoken of my resilience, and great sense of adventure and love of life. I accept those sentiments as a fitting testament to the foundation of the person I have grown to be.

Acknowledgements

I dedicate this book to my grandchildren and all the children I have cared for during my career. Hoping they will be inspired to grasp every opportunity to reach their full potential and be happy.

Thank you to Barnardo's for rescuing me and four of my siblings and archiving my records for nearly fifty years.

A special thank you for the warm welcome I received when, 'visiting my past' which in turn motivated me to capture my childhood memoirs on paper.

Appreciation and thanks, to the members of Bennet House Writers group, who have given me support and guidance during my journey writing this book. I could not have managed without them.

Thank you to family and friends for their encouragement, patience and reassurance, 'You can do it.'

Last but not least, a huge thank you to my valued friends who have helped me with IT skills and, proofreading my manuscript, with their knowledge and wisdom they advised me the best way forward.